BURRILLVILLE
(Rhode Island)

As It Was
and As It Is

1856

Horace A. Keach

HERITAGE BOOKS
2024

HERITAGE BOOKS
AN IMPRINT OF HERITAGE BOOKS, INC.

Books, CDs, and more—Worldwide

For our listing of thousands of titles see our website
at
www.HeritageBooks.com

Published 2024 by
HERITAGE BOOKS, INC.
Publishing Division
5810 Ruatan Street
Berwyn Heights, MD 20740

This work was originally published in 1856 and has been re-typeset and indexed by Patricia A. Mehrtens for this volume.

All rights reserved. No part of this book may be reproduced or transmitted in any form or by any means, electronic or mechanical, including photocopying, recording or by any information storage and retrieval system without written permission from the author, except for the inclusion of brief quotations in a review.

International Standard Book Number
Paperbound: 978-1-55613-536-1

To
GEN. ELISHA DYER,
by whose liberality and patronage the
statistics of Burrillville were
collected,
This work is respectfully dedicated,
by his friend, the Author

PREFACE

This volume, about the past and present of my native town, was penned during a few weeks of recreative leisure in the summer of 1856. In a rural district there are no centers of information, few and meager public records, and no historic compilations to which one can resort for aid. A chaos of poor traditions is to be reduced to order, and incoherent chronicles of popular events arranged to tell their story as time told it.

I have said nothing in regard to the original purchases of our land from the Indians. I preferred to leave it until I could include a larger territory. Those purchases often included tracts that were lying in several towns, and their importance demands a more elaborate notice, than would seem consistent with a sketch of so small a portion of north western Rhode Island. The same remark will apply to the long controversy about the west line.

I have not found anything printed in relation to Burrillville except ephemeral sketches which I prepared a few years ago for the Providence Journal. The command of Sydney's muse was "Look into thy heart and write." I have followed a like impulse, which will account for the prominence given to the subject of Reforms. My fellow citizens, who love our town will rejoice with me at all signs of progress, and strangers who ask what we have in Burrillville, will be glad to learn of our prosperity. To record our gradual but sure advancement, has been to me a pleasure, and my humble labor done, I commend it to the favor of an indulgent public.

THE AUTHOR (Horace A. Keach)
Burrillville, Oct. 1, 1856.

Burrillville: As It Was and As It Is by Horace A. Keach 1856

CONTENTS

CHAPTER I
Tradition

Few traces of the Indians—the Nipmucs—Pas-co-ag—Black Hut—Herring Pond Woods—Indian Barbarities—Indian Skeleton eight feet high—Indian Cornfield and Wigwam—Mehunganug Swamp—Comb Basket one hundred and fifty years old - - - - Page 9

CHAPTER II
The Wilderness

Two hundred and twenty years ago—John Smith—The Williams Family—Deer—Fish from the sea—Wolf Pits—Early Settlement in Herring Pond Woods -Page 13

CHAPTER III
Old Times

Shay's Rebellion—Taxes and Tories—Primitive Customs—Old Burrillville Meeting House - Page 17

CHAPTER IV
Old Places

Money Rocks—Snake Dens—Smith Battey's Diamonds Bark Mill and Turning Lathe—The Old Paul House - - - - - - - - - - - - Page 22

CHAPTER V
Natural History

Animated Nature—Little Birds—Bald Eagle — Rattlesnakes —White Squirrel -Page 26

Burrillville: As It Was and As It Is by Horace A. Keach 1856

CHAPTER VI
Glocester and Its Division

Burrillville a part of Providence—Burrillville included in Glocester—Corn in the Town Treasury—Petition to divide the town—Petition granted, and Act passed—Another vote to divide Glocester -Page 28

CHAPTER VII
Modern Legislation

Hon. James Burrill—Books presented to the town—Vote to pay Grand Committee—first Taxes—Sale of the Poor—Sale of the Town Meeting—Town Council sold—Extra pay to the soldiers of 1812 — Sale of the Town Meeting becomes a nuisance —A thwack at Office Seekers —Small Pox in 1825 —A slice from Glocester in 1844 — The License Question— Fiftieth birthday of Burrillville - - - - Page 32

CHAPTER VIII
Old Men

The Harringtons—Joktan Putnam—Captain William Rhodes—Our Mysterious Visitor (The Darned Man) - - - - - - - - - - - - - - - Page 36

CHAPTER IX
Internal Improvements

The roads of Burrillville—"The Air Line"—"The indomitable Mac" —The Woonasquatucket- -Page 38

CHAPTER X
Education

Old Schoolhouses—Mutiny—Smashing Windows—Hon. Henry Barnard —School District Boundaries —Rude Boys and smiling School Marms—Libraries—Decision under the School Law -Page 41

CHAPTER XI
Temperance

Old Drinking customs—Washingtonianism—The Honest Quaker — Temperance Songs—Dr. Harrington and his trial—Harvey P. Brown —The Main Law—Round Top—Singular Outrage, destruction of books—Extract from our "Scrap Book"—The Wreckers - - - Page 45

CHAPTER XII
Freedom

Fugitive Slave Law in Burrillville—Slaves at work in Herring Pond Woods-"Jack's Grave"-Women's Rights-Angel's Visits - - - - Page 52

CHAPTER XIII
Religion

Eld. John Colby's mission to Burrillville —First F. B. Church in Rhode Island—Clarissa Danforth—First Pastor—Millerism—Church meeting in the Esten neighborhood—Smith's Academy— Liberality of Nicholas Brown—"New Lights"—Huntsville Emporium—Methodists—Church of England—Friends—Universalists - -Page 55

CHAPTER XIV
Nature

Divining Rods —Wallum Lake —Bathing Beach —A race through Wallum Lake—Canal company claim the Lake —Largest forest in RI—Winter scene on Buck Hill—September Gale — Apples "from a tree that fell 40 years ago"—Southern Pictures- - - - - - - - - -Page 62

CHAPTER XV
Factories

Burrillville Cotton Gin—The first factory—Old Burrillville Bank—Mapleville -Page 67

CHAPTER XVI
The Present

Our Climate—Changes in the Seasons—Employments— Land at 12 1/2 cents per acre—Two dozen factories—"Five miles to the store"—"Away to school"—Our buildings—"The nicely sanded floor"—Wooden Clocks—Our Parlors—Barns—Wood piles—Living out in the lots— Rhode Island Brown Bread—A good Dinner—The Farmer's dress —Factory Girls —Books — "Such a nice carriage"—Parties—"Ring Plays" and "Round the Chimney"—Sleigh Rides —Quilting Bees —Husking Frolic — Rabbit Hunting — Going to the Shore — At rest, at last. -Page 70

SUPPLEMENT - Page 81

INDEX -Page 94

Burrillville: As It Was and As It Is by Horace A. Keach 1856

INTRODUCTION

Important Political and Social Influences of the Institution of the Township

The following are the observations of M. DeTocqueville upon the American system of municipal bodies. Ideas are presented that will be new to some and interesting to all. The author was a member of the Institute of France and of the Chamber of Deputies, and his admirable work upon the Political Institutions of America has attracted attention, not only in our country, but throughout Europe. We may here remark that the counties of our northern States are divided into Towns, those of the southern into Parishes. There are many regulations which belong exclusively to our New England towns, and the peculiar municipal franchises of the North have not been without important social results.

"The village or township is the only association which is so perfectly natural that wherever a number are men are collected, it seems to constitute itself. The town or tithing, as the smallest division of a community, must necessarily exist in all nations, whatever their laws and customs may be; if man makes monarchies and establishes republics, the first association of mankind seems constituted by the hand of God. But although the existence of the township is coeval with that of man, its liberties are not the less rarely respected and easily destroyed. A nation is always able to establish great political assemblies because it habitually contains a certain number of individuals fitted by their talents, if not by their habits, for the direction of affairs. The township is, on the contrary, composed of coarser materials which are less easily fashioned by the legislator. The difficulties which attend the consolidation of its independence rather augment than diminish with the increasing enlightenment of the people. A highly-civilized community spurns the attempts of a local independence, is disgusted at its numerous blunders, and is apt to despair of success before the experiment is completed.

"Again, no immunities are so ill-protected from the encroachments of the supreme power as those of municipal bodies in general; they are unable to struggle single-handed against a strong or an enterprising government, and they cannot defend their cause with success unless it be identified with the customs of the nation and supported by public opinion. Thus, until the independence of townships is amalgamated with the manners of a people, it is easily destroyed; and it is only after a long existence in the laws that it can be thus amalgamated. Municipal freedom eludes the exertions of man; it is rarely created; but it is as it were, secretly and spontaneously engendered in the midst of a semi-barbarous state of society. The constant action of the laws and the national habits, peculiar circumstances, and above all, time, may consolidate it; but there is certainly no nation on the continent of Europe which has experienced its advantages. Nevertheless, local assemblies of citizens constitute the strength of free nations. Municipal institutions are to liberty what primary schools are to science; they bring it within the people's reach, they teach men how to use and how to enjoy it. A nation may establish a system of free government, but without the spirit of municipal institutions it cannot have the spirit of liberty. The transient passions and the interests of an hour or the change of circumstances may have created the external forms of independence; but the despotic tendency which has been repelled will, sooner or later, inevitably reappear on the surface. In the township as well as everywhere else, the people is the only source of power; but in no stage of the government does the body of citizens exercise a more immediate influence. In America the people is a master whose exigencies demand obedience to the utmost limits of possibility.

"Municipal independence is a natural consequence of the principle of the sovereignty of the people in the United States: all the American republics recognize it more or less; but circumstances have peculiarly favored its growth in New England. In this part of the Union, the impulsion of political activity was given in the townships; and it may almost be said that each formed an independent nation. When the kings of England asserted their supremacy, they were contented to assume the central power of the state. The townships of New England remained as they were before; and although they were now subject to the state, they were at first scarcely dependent upon it. It is important to remember that they have not been invested with privileges, but they seem, on the contrary, to have surrendered a portion of their independence to the state. The townships are only subordinate to the state in those interests which I shall term *social*, as they are common to all the citizens. They are independent in all that concerns themselves; and among all the inhabitants of New England, I believe that not a man is to be found who would acknowledge that the state has any right to interfere in the local interests. The towns of New England buy and sell, prosecute or are indicted, augment or diminish their rates, without the slightest opposition on the part of the administrative authority of the state.

"They are bound however, to comply with the demands of the community. If the state is in the need of money, a town can neither give nor withhold supplies. If the state projects a road, the township cannot refuse to let it cross its territory. If a police regulation is made by the state, it must be enforced by the town. A uniform system of instruction is organized all over the state, and every town is bound to establish the schools which the law ordains. The New Englander is attached to his township, not only because he was born in it but because it constitutes a strong and free social body of which he is a member and whose government claims and deserves the exercise of his sagacity.

"In Europe the absence of local spirit is a frequent subject of regret to those who are in power; every one agrees that there is no surer guarantee of order and tranquility, and yet nothing is more difficult to create. If the municipal bodies were made powerful and independent, the authorities of the nation might be disunited and the peace of the country endangered. Yet, without power and independence, a town may contain good subjects, but it can have no active citizens.

"Another important fact is that the township of New England is so constituted as to excite the warmest of human affections without arousing the ambitious passions of the heart of man. The officers of the county are not elected and their authority is very limited. Even the state is only a second-rate community whose tranquil and obscure administration offers no inducement sufficient to draw men away from the circle of their interests into the turmoil of public affairs. The federal government confers power and honor on the men who conduct it; but those individuals can never be very numerous. The high station of the presidency can only be reached at an advanced period of life; and the other federal functionaries are generally men who have been favored by fortune or distinguished in some other career. Such cannot be the permanent aim of the ambitious.

"But the township is a center for the desire of public esteem, the want of exciting interests, and the taste for authority and popularity in the midst of the ordinary relations of life; and the passions which commonly embroil society change their character when they find a vent so near the domestic hearth and the family circle. In the American states, power has been disseminated with admirable skill for the purpose of interesting the greatest possible number of persons in the public weal. Independently of the electors who are from time to time called into action, the body politic is divided into innumerable functionaries and officers who all, in their several spheres, represent the same powerful corporation in whose name they act. The local administration thus affords an unfailing source of profit and interest to a vast number of individuals.

"The American system, which divides the local authority among so many citizens, does not scruple to multiply the functions of the town officers. For in the United States it is believed, and with truth, that patriotism is a kind of devotion which is strengthened by ritual observance. In this manner, the activity of the township is continually perceptible; it is daily manifested in the fulfillment of a duty or the exercise of a right; and a constant though gentle motion is thus kept up in society which animates without disturbing it.

The American attaches himself to his home as the mountaineer clings to his hills, because the characteristic features of his country are there more distinctly marked than elsewhere. The existence of the township of new England is in general a happy one. Their government is suited to their taste and chosen by themselves. In the midst of the profound peace and general comfort which reign in America; the commotions of municipal discord are infrequent. The conduct of local business is easy. The political education of the people has long been complete; say rather that it was complete when the people first set foot upon the soil.

"In New England no tradition exists of a distinction of ranks; no portion of the community is tempted to oppress the remainder; and the abuses which may injure isolated individuals are forgotten in the general contentment which prevails.

"If the government is defective, (and it would no doubt be easy to point out its deficiencies) the fact that it really emanates from those it governs and that it acts, either ill or well, casts the protecting spell of a parental pride over all its faults. No term of comparison disturbs the satisfaction of the citizen; England formerly governed the mass of the colonies, but the people were always sovereign in the township where their rule is not only an ancient but a primitive state.

"The native of New England is attached to his township because it is independent; and his cooperation in its affairs ensures his attachment to its interest; the well-being it affords him secures his affection; and its welfare is the aim of his ambition and of his future exertions; he takes a part in every occurrence in the place; he practices the art of government in the small sphere within his reach; he accustoms himself to those forms which can alone ensure the steady progress of liberty; he imbibes their spirit; he acquires a taste for order, comprehends the union of the balance of powers, and collects clear practical notions of the nature of his duties and the extent of his rights."

Burrillville: As It Was and As It Is by Horace A. Keach 1856

CHAPTER 1
Tradition

The Town of Burrillville lies in the extreme northwestern corner of the state of Rhode Island. It is in latitude 42 degrees, and about twenty miles from the city of Providence.

The adjacent towns upon the north are Douglas and Uxbridge in Massachusetts, on the east is the ancient town of Smithfield, Glocester lies along its southern border, and Thompson in Connecticut is upon the west. It is of this territory, comprising an area of fifty-three and two-tenths square miles, that we propose to give the history.

The lapse of two centuries and a quarter, since this region was first claimed by the whites, has obliterated most traces of the aboriginal inhabitants. Now and then the farmer's plow turns up some rude weapon of Indian warfare, or broken fragments of their domestic utensil. Their hunting grounds are forsaken, their cabins are decayed, and only purblind tradition tells where they once stood.

But while Wallum Lake smiles among our northern hills, and the Chepachet and Pas-coag flow through our valleys, they will never be forgotten. Their language is linked with the beautiful brooks, whose silvery cascades brighten our hillsides, and it is graven on the imperishable granite of the craggy battlements that will forever frown over Saxonvale.

At the time our State was settled, the region about here was occupied by the Nipmuc Indians. The country was called the Nipmuc dominion. This tribe were tributary to the Narragansetts, but took advantage of the arrival of the English to shake off their dependence. When King Philip, the sachem of the Narragansetts, from his seat on Mount Hope, heard of their defection, he was surrounded by so many bitter and implacable enemies, that he could spare no warriors to bring back the deserting tribe to their allegiance.

There is a stream in the northern part of Burrillville that has always been called the Nipmuc River. Certain lands, devised in the will of John Inman, an old settler here, are bounded by the "Nipmuc." The river is formed by the union of three little rills. One rises in Shockalog Swamp in Uxbridge, Massachusetts, one in Baiting Pond in Douglas, and the other has its source in Maple Sap Swamp. The river formed by these flows southerly through the

Arnold and D. Salisbury estate, running through a wood called the Pine Swamp, and uniting with Clear River at Shippee Bridge.

There was another tribe called Pas-co-ag Indians. One of our chief villages still retains this name. It is a ledgey place, and furnishes among the rocks around, a secure retreat for snakes. In the Indian dialect, the term "coag" meant a snake, and when they went by this locality they said "Pass Coag."

The Mohawk Indians, prior to the old French War, were often basking about this region, visiting their relatives among our tribes, and uniting with them in trapping the Otter on the banks of the Iron Mine and Round Pond Brook.

On the farm once called the "David Inman Place," now owned by Smith Wood, Esq., was a cabin called by the old settlers the "Black Hut." This was always supposed to be an old Indian wigwam. From this settlement they could readily fish in Herring Pond or Clear River, or hunt in the extensive adjacent forest.

At the first settlement around Herring Pond the whites found only saplings in the woods. There were a few great chestnuts and oaks, but the Indians had set fires in the forests, and our ancestors fed their cattle upon the wild grass that readily sprung from the charred soil. Like most frontier settlements, the hamlets of the early pioneers in these northwestern woods were exposed to the incursions of the ruthless savages. Their dwellings were furnished with embrasures, and a constant guard was kept against the cunning tactics of the red men. But the danger could not always be averted, and the horrid war-whoop sometimes sounded at midnight around the burning home of some white family. Mothers with their infants fell beneath the tomahawk, and strong men were struck down while bravely defending their hearthstones.

Those were still more unfortunate who were preserved alive. After long and weary marches to reach some Pequod or Mohegan village, the miserable captives perished under barbarous torture. Friendly visitors from the Nipmuc tribe found the habitations of their allies a blackened heap of ruins. Those who left the settlement at Providence to visit their friends on the verge of the wilderness broke their hearts when told that they had fallen victims to the murderous vengeance of the savage foe.

We who live in these peaceful times have ever been strangers to the hardships and dangers of border life. Our dwellings are unguarded, and our lives and property secure. Our ancestors had the poisoned arrow and the crimsoned tomahawk without and fears and terror within, while we, who dwell on the sites of their fallen settlements, have none to molest or make us afraid. The danger is past. Tales of sanguinary warfare may occupy a winter's evening, but the terrific reality threatens no more. Tis only like the memory of some horrid dream.

Burrillville: As It Was and As It Is by Horace A. Keach 1856

A few years ago a discovery was made by one of our citizens which reveals the physical character of those with whom our ancestors had to contend. In 1836, Capt. Samuel White, in excavating beneath his wood house, found the remains of a human skeleton of proportions altogether unlike our modern inhabitants. He called several of his neighbors to view it and among them was Doctor Levi Eddy. The body was lying upon the side with arms folded, head bent forward, and the knees drawn upward. It was exhumed, the bones were put together, and all parties were surprised at its gigantic height. After surveying it awhile, the Doctor exclaimed, "He was a bouncer! He must have been as much as eight feet high." Was he some tall sachem that ruled in the Nipmuc forest before the Pilgrim Fathers landed at Plymouth? Had he fallen in the chase, was he shot down by a hidden foe, or was this the site of a battlefield, where he fell shouting his warriors on to the conflict? Tradition is silent; echo has no answer.

At the base of Snake Hill is a field that has always been called the "Indian's Cornfield." Here were little mounds where it appeared the Indians planted their Maize, putting it in the same hill each year. The hills are much larger than the "Indian Hills" of the whites, which they make when they sow rye among their corn at the last hoeing. The points were much further apart than our present mode of planting. It is now overflowed by a Factory Pond.

Upon the lower part of the farm now occupied by Nelson Armstrong, Esq., are the remains of an Indian Wigwam. Within the memory of Moses Cooper, who died in 1837 age ninety-five, there was a wigwam there, but it has crumbled away and there is only a pile of stones left. These are supposed to be the material of their chimney.

Here in the valley, sheltered from the winds and near the confluence of the "Chepa's Sack? and "Clear" was a good location. The Indians have always been noted for the selection of the best sites and for hunting and fishing, this would be a convenient situation.

In the Mehunganug Swamp are Cedars more than two hundred years old, counting by the grains. In these are found a great many bullets. When the largest cedar logs are sawed, bullets are taken out near the heart. If these were shot into the young trees by hunters, it must have been when game was larger than at present, for most of our sportsmen now use shot for the rabbits, squirrels, and "such small deer."

There is a rumor of a fight between the Whites and Indians at this place, but when we were told that it was with the Narragansett Tribe, we thought our informant might have confounded it with the "Swamp Fight" on the banks of the Miskianza or Chickaseen river in the western part of the town of South Kingston.

Deacon Duty Salisbury, the oldest man in our town at

present, has a comb basket or case given to his mother by the Indians of Metaka woods. It is woven like a basket and must be at least one hundred and fifty years old.

About thirty years ago, while the Deacon was digging for a gate post, he found a bundle of arrows and several other implements. They were in a pile together about two feet under ground. One of those was composed of a Porphyritic stone of a character unlike any at present to be found in this vicinity. These scanty relics are all that we can now discover of the aboriginal race. Again, we regret that in our town the record of legendary lore is so barren of romantic incident. Through what mutations did that race pass who were dominant here three hundred years since?

Man loves the spot that gave him birth. The Switzer clings to his mountain home; old Scocia's hills are vocal with the songs of Burns in their praise, who joined with the immortal Scott in poetic worship of "the land of the mountain and the flood;" England, "Merrie England" has patriot peasant and cultured scholars on the banks of the Avon and the margin of the Thames, who love the hallowed memories that are woven into the lovely scenes of their native land.

In our New England homes we love to look out over the valleys and up to the hills that claim our reverence by virtue of the great deeds enacted in their presence. And as we walk through the glens or look from the hilltops of our native town, we sigh that there is no story of the life and love, of the strong free men, and the dark-eyed maidens who worshiped the Great Spirit beneath these skies three centuries ago.

Burrillville: As It Was and As It Is by Horace A. Keach 1856

CHAPTER II
The Wilderness

    Two hundred and twenty years have gone by since the axe of the palefaces startled echoes in the forest of the Nipmuc, and the wilderness has been made to "blossom like the rose." The Indians have disappeared and the whirr of the spindle and the din of the factory bells tell us the Anglo Saxons rule here. The smoke from the red man's cabin no longer curls above our pine treetops and the chiefs who ruled in northern Rhode Island have gone to sleep with their fathers.

    It was not long after the settlement of Providence before the whites made inroads upon the wilderness in this direction. John Smith came from the northern part of that settlement with his axe and wallet of victuals, and felling trees across the streams, he traversed the woods till he came to a spot near what is now called the "Tar Kiln Saw Mill." Here he found the stream—on which several mills have since been built—and thinking it a good site, concluded to settle there. He looked the forest over, going out into Horse Head Woods and around the foot of Den Hill, but at last pitched upon a spot in the side of a hill near where the Urania Smith house now stands. When his victuals were gone he went back to the city, and his brother and several other adventurers came out with him. The spot they had selected was sheltered from the winds and water was easily had from the brook nearby. There was game in the forest then, and they managed to live by an occasional visit to the city until they had made a clearing and the yellow maize gave them the staff of life. At one time almost all that part of the town was occupied by the Smith family. They are all descendants of the hardy pioneer who felled the first tree and built the first cabin in East Burrillville.

    There is a family in our town who trace their pedigree directly to the founder of Rhode Island. Rufus Williams, Esq. dwells on the site of the old house erected by his ancestors when the settlement at Providence was new. Belonging to the original farm was a large part of the land that now constitutes four. Two large oaks that tradition has assigned for part of its boundary have been felled within twenty years. The old house stood a few feet to the west of the present one, just at the edge of the garden. No vestige of it now remains.

Burrillville: As It Was and As It Is by Horace A. Keach 1856

When the forest was but partially cleared, our ancestors must have derived a great portion of the subsistence from the animals then abundant. They depended much upon venison. In A. D. 1728 in the reign of King George the Second, the colony made a law to preserve deer in this State. No deer were to be killed between January and June. A violation of this decree was punished by a fine of thirty dollars.

To a citizen of this modern town, it will not seem improbable when we suggest that the last deer of Rhode Island was shot on the margin of Wallum Lake. The hunter who pursues a few half starved rabbits among the bushes in the northern part of the town is vexed as he remembers that the lofty hill that lifts its bosky summit above Eagle Peak has always been called Buck Hill. If he could see the red deer bound along the banks of Pascoag river or dash through Douglas woods, he would be better paid for his toilsome sport. The prowess of our factory boys now manifests itself in a terrible slaughter of chipmunks and pigeon woodpeckers, it may be with the same old iron bound smooth bore that their ancestors used to shoot Nipmucs and black bears.

The only deer that has been seen in Burrillville within the memory of the "oldest inhabitant," was a tame one owned by Captain William Rhodes. He placed it in the center of a load of goods giving it a chance to put its head out; and so it was brought from Providence to Rhodesville. For many years it was kept upon his premises and was a great curiosity to the country people, many of whom had never seen a menagerie.

There is a man at Brandy Hill in Thompson, Connecticut, whose grandfather told him about seeing deer in that region. They came out upon the plains between the Wallum Lake woods and the hill. A man in the eastern part of our town who is himself old tells us what the old people used to tell him about the animals of those parts. One man saw nine deer at one time run out from a clump of wood near what is now called Mount Pleasant and he could watch the tossing of their antlers but a few moments before they were so far down the valley as to be lost to his view.

Many years ago before the factory dams were built, certain kinds of fish came up our streams in the Spring to deposit their spawn in our ponds and in the Fall the new stock would descent to the sea. Alewives and Herring were among the varieties, and one of our ponds still bears the name of Herring Pond. Sometimes they have been known to fill the streams at the fording-places so that it was difficult to cross while the shoal was passing. They were taken by the farmers in considerable quantities and used as fertilizers.

Since the factories were built here, our stock in the rivers is limited. In the ponds the sport is better. An expert can get a "mess" in a short time in Wallum Lake or Sucker Pond, but the "fisherman's luck" of those not used to it is small. Sometimes when "it rains so hard we cannot work" we take a boat and frequent the coves of those ponds, and a full string rewards us for our pains.

There were once wolves in Burrillville. There are "wolf pits" on the west of Paulson's shingle mill. The old settlers used to trap them by digging deep pits, with the bottom full of sharp stakes, and the surface lightly covered and well baited. A hill in this region still retains the name of "Wolf Hill."

The Salsbury family were among the first who settled in the central parts of Burrillville. Edward Salsbury, the father of Duty Salsbury of Pascoag, was formerly a resident of Smithfield, R. I. He enlisted in the old French War with the assurance that he would not be called upon to leave the town; but his regiment was soon ordered to New York, and out to Lake Erie. He was engaged in building Fort Stanwix. He carefully saved his wages, and at the close of the war purchased three hundred acres of land on the east side of Herring Pond. Not a rood of it was cleared. He built a rude cabin and removed his family to it. Duty Salsbury remembers when they come across the Branch Bridge in a cart drawn by oxen. There were no wagons then and those who had horses only used them with the saddle. The boy sat at his mother's feet and his father guided the oxen along the rude paths until they come to the solitary hut which was to be their future home. There were five other children, and these trudged along in sturdy defiance of bushes and brakes.

A little spot was cleared around their cabin; they had one cow; the woods supplied them with game and the pond with fish. The Revolutionary war began. Edward Salsbury had six bushels of corn. He took this to Hunt's mill at the place now called Round Top, and brought home six bushels of meal. A day had scarcely past when three guns were fired at Providence, and answered at various points, until the echoes went over Herring Woods. They were the alarm guns to call the minute men. The woodman must lay by his axe and shoulder his musket. Edward, taking a hasty farewell of his family, telling them he did not know when he could return, if ever, and bidding them be frugal of their little stock of provisions, shouldered his knapsack and joined his comrades in arms. For six weeks the family lived on such food as could be prepared from Indian meal, with salt and water, for their cow was dry. When they had milk they fared much better for they could then have "hasty pudding, pudding and milk, and milk porridge."

Twenty years later the youngest boy whom we now call "Deacon," (he holds that office in the Baptist Church) left the homestead and moved to the place now called Pascoag. It is almost seventy years ago that he began to battle with the wilderness there. Now there are seven factories in a circuit of a mile, coaches run through the valley where he snared the first partridge, and the mason's hammer rings on the ledge where the fox hid himself from the pioneer's rifle. Nothing remains of the old, save the rocky hill whose thunder splintered battlements seem to fortify the village and the name the Indian gave to the river and the valley.

We shall never forget the worthy Deacon with his silver hair, stern independence, and sturdy piety. His stereotyped exhortation of "I believe religion is a good thing, the Lord has been good to me," has been repeated for three-fourths of a century, and now, in his second childhood, he repeats it still.

CHAPTER III
Old Times

That resistance to legal authority that finally ripened into the "Shay's Rebellion," was commenced in Burrillville. There was a class at the revolution called reformation men, who would not fight, and refused to pay the onerous taxes imposed to defray the expenses of the war.

One day an officer, with three men to aid him, distrained some cattle belonging to farmers in the neighborhood of what is now called the Phillips place. A mob was formed to rescue them. The officers were pursued and overtaken just as they crossed the bridge to the N. E. of Pascoag village. Beyond the bridge was a dense wood. Here commenced a scuffle, the farmers well knowing that if the cattle went over the bridge some of them would be carried away. The officers were overpowered and the animals were driven back to the farm yards. My informant stood by and saw it all. He was a lad of thirteen then and in the employ of the man resident on the Phillips place.

The next morning an officer called upon the principal conspirator. The officer was a well known neighbor and not being suspected was welcomed into the house. "Have you any tobacco?" asked the agent of the powers that were. "By the Lord! no," was the reply of the insurgent who answered with his favorite phrase; but he said he would call his fellow, he believed he had some. The comrade was called and here the rest of the officials rushed in and the chiefs were taken. There were two of them. Four more were soon secured and they were marched to Chepachet to undergo an examination. The people of the vicinity assembled and followed them, intending to rescue them as they had their property. An eye witness says he "never saw so many folks in Chepachet except in the Dorr time." The mob entered the Court Room and set the prisoners free. A messenger was sent to consult Judge Steere. He was a man of considerable influence and a resident not far from Chepachet. Said he to the nuncio, "I must see the Governor." The Judge ordered his horse and posted to Providence to lay the case before Governor Fenner. This was not the only time that news was to be carried to the occupant of the gubernatorial chair that treason was rampant in Chepachet.

Burrillville: As It Was and As It Is by Horace A. Keach 1856

The Governor sent a message to the leaders of the rioters that if they would proceed no further the past should be overlooked. The amnesty was accepted, but it did not prevent the occurrence of another riot soon after. Several were arrested and lodged in the State Jail, but they were soon released. The excitement went over the border. A fight with fists and clubs took place in Douglas, and in the western and northern towns of Massachusetts, powder and balls were used. But after the defeat of Daniel Shays, who took the lead of the movement in that State, the riotous proceedings abated.

In those days there were many tories. No man knew who might be his enemy. the officers often abused their authority. The taxes were exorbitant, but the extortions of the tax gatherers were a greater grievance. A cow would be sold at auction to pay a tax, and if it brought fifteen silver dollars, the State might get five, the officer five, and five paid the bye-bidder. The same animal would bring one hundred dollars of the paper continental currency. The people had been often cheated. The large woods, now called the "Pine Woods," east of Harrisville, was once sold for fifteen hundred dollars of the continental money, but a tender being made of a pair of oxen, the lot was regarded as paid for.

John Inman the first, as he was called, could point to twenty cows in his yard when the war began. At its close he had but one. A gray-haired farmer tells us, he has killed a calf, tied the meat in a bag and slinging it across his horse's back, gone through the woods a score of miles to the city of Providence and sold it to get money to help pay his taxes. We, of later days, know little of the privations of those who lived in "the times that tried men's souls," and who have cleared the forests, dammed the streams, and fenced the land, for their less hardy descendants.

Perhaps such brief review as we may be able to give of the customs of our ancestors may not be altogether uninteresting. No record has ever been collated that gave us an account of the manners and habits of the primitive inhabitants of Burrillville, and what little we have been able to gather of ancient modes of living has been by transient conversation with our old people, and the hereditary rumors of traditional gossip. We have enjoyed the privilege of several conversations with Deacon Duty Salisbury, whose great age and very excellent memory well fit him for a review of long ago. The Deacon's father could remember when there was but one house from Providence bridge to Olneyville.

The men of those olden times were much larger than most of our young men. Their stalwart forms would present quite a contrast with the trim appearance of their degenerate posterity. Among the amusements of olden times were trials of strength in various ways. Lifting, wrestling, or mowing were some of the modes by which those feats were performed.

Burrillville: As It Was and As It Is by Horace A. Keach 1856

Most of the inhabitants of Burrillville will remember Otis Wood, Esq., one of the men who in his massive physical proportions resembled the old settlers. He was once at a Cattle Fair at Worcester, Mass., where the power of a yoke of oxen to sustain a weight upon their necks had been tested by attaching them to a cart heavily loaded with stones. The oxen were detached and several men in the crowd tried to lift the cart-tongue with the stones still aboard. No single man had done it. Otis stepped forward, and putting his brawny hands under it, took it right up. "Where did you come from?" was the inquiry on all sides. "From Burrillville, in Rhode Island." "Have you any more men like yourself down there?" "Oh, yes! Some who are a good deal stouter than I am." "Well, we don"t want to see them, then."

In those days of giants, Esek Phetteplace was considered the stoutest man in town. These great men loved to exhibit their power. If they heard of a rival anywhere, they would take some pains to meet him. I have heard an old man tell of those matches among the old wrestlers. At one time, Paul Dudley took hold with Stout Raymond. The place where they met was upon a barn floor. The scaffolds on either side were covered with eager and noisy partisans. Brandy was esteemed a luxury then, and at these gladiatorial combats, all hands were merry. Dudley "filed" his opponent, which sporting term then meant, bringing him upon his knees. Dudley's admirers hurrahed, and the friends of Stout Raymond clenched their teeth as they intently watched the scuffle. Again Raymond got "filed." The spectators crowded to the edge of the scaffold to peer over upon the combatants and swear their defiance at the opposite party. Raymond's case looked doubtful for "three files made a throw," and the powerful Dudley, stimulated by his success, grasped him with confidence. In a moment Raymond was stretched at full length upon the threshing floor. The scaffolds were instantly cleared, the men of each party attacked the others, and a furious and bloody medley ensued. Such were the brutal pastimes in this portion of the "Plantations," among the rough old settlers who had developed their burly strength by wrestling with our forest oaks.

At the period that succeeded the Revolution, the food of the people here was coarser than at present. They had enough, but it was not tortured into the unhealthy compounds that modern cookery has devised to the ruin of the human stomach. Boys and girls grew fat on mush and milk, our grandmothers relished their own home-brewed and brown bread, and our sturdy paternal grand ancestors became tall and stout by virtue of pork and beans.

When the war broke out, they were deprived of the few foreign luxuries they had before enjoyed. They could get no tea and they found a substitute in a beverage made from Red Root, sometimes called Even Root. They made sage tea, and from the

Burrillville: As It Was and As It Is by Horace A. Keach 1856

inside bark of the chestnut they prepared a kind of chocolate. While our brave sires were on the field of battle, their wives at home were gossiping patriotically as they sipped a beverage for which they thanked no British king.

Our men in those times wore a sort of pants called "Petticoat Trousers." They are sometimes seen now upon the stage. What would one of our modern fops think, could he meet a fine gentleman of the old school, with his small clothes, bright shoe buckles, military plackets and powdered wig. The ladies could not indulge in the fashionable finery of modern extravagance. The first calico gown worn in Burrillville was the acquisition of a belle of Pascoag, a sister of Duty Salisbury. Calico was calico in those days. Ten acres of land would be given for a single dress.

It may seem superfluous to refer to the hooped petticoats, once so fashionable among the dames of Burrillville. We have seen the custom as large as life. Our modern maids and matrons have rustled through our drawing rooms and promenaded our streets, in all the munificence of the antique garb while we demurely whispered: "Can such things be, and overcome us like a summer cloud, without our special wonder?" The shoes of the girls of 1750 were made of velvet, and sometimes of a stuff called durant. They were homemade. They would tie them in their pocket handkerchiefs when they went on meeting, and put them on when almost there. Many old women went all the way barefoot.

Men rode much on horseback in those days. They learned their horses to pace, and their gentle gait would be as easy as a cradle. There were no wagons here then, and on Sunday morning John and Judy would mount the same horse and jog away to church, conversing in friendly phrase, as man and wife should. A modern riding-dress would have cost a farm. When men began to "wait for the wagon" they took pains to break up the racking gait of their low-stepping nags. They would place rails in their path, twenty feet apart. These would compel them to abandon their shuffle trot and pick up their limbs as the steeds of our day do.

The dwellers in the east part of Burrillville two hundred years ago lived in log huts. Old John Esten had a log house in the neighborhood where a number of families of this name still reside. It was all woods, and the woods were full of bears. There were only small clearings around each hut, and the gun and fishing rod were used as often as the hoe and axe.

The food of the pioneers was of the coarsest quality. They often made bean porridge, a dish never tasted by this generation. The old pantry chorus: "Bean Porridge hot, and bean porridge cold. Bean Porridge best when nine days old" is oblivious of meaning to the moderns. Sometimes this plural aliment became sour, then old Zebedee Hopkins used to boil walnut chips with them, "to sweeten 'em." People were "ruggeder then than they are now." Mr. John Esten made chocolate of maple sap. The trees grew by a brook near the residence of George Walling, Esq. When the maple sap ceased running, he boiled maple bark to make his daily beverage.

Among the first wants of the new settlers was a place for public worship. The few who had not imbibed the infidel sentiments, so prevalent during the war, were desirous of erecting a church. The first church was built by the Freewill Baptists. A lottery was instituted and the proceeds devoted to the erection of the building. It is now used for our Town House, but for a great many years it was called the "Burrillville Freewill Baptist Meeting House." It was apparent that the revenue from the lottery would not complete the edifice, and a subscription was set on foot. They had not agreed upon its location. The dwellers at Rhodesville wanted it at that place; the people around Pascoag would like to have it nearer them. It was at last decided that the side of the river where the people subscribed the largest sum should have the house. The greatest amount was obtained upon the west side, and the house was begun.

When raised and partly covered, the funds gave out, and the work stopped for some years. Another effort was made to finish the lower part, but when half the pews were up, the exchequer was again empty, and the Society offered to give Deacon Salisbury the upper story if he would finish the house. He was a carpenter, had a saw-mill near Pascoag, owned plenty of timber, and he accepted the offer. A high steeple was first put upon it, but about 1812 it was found to be leaky around it and it was sawed off. A great crowd gathered to see it come down. A long rope was attached to it, hundreds of hands seized it, and it came to the ground with a crash that splintered it into kindling wood. When it fell it reached almost to the road, which those who have been by there will remember, is a good way from the house. The house was covered anew and the porch built to it. A few years later, it was offered to the town upon condition that they would keep the outside in repair. The inside is a curiosity. There is a lofty pulpit above which is a painting representing cherubim, but a most rude and shabby daub. The pews are square pens with seats on the four sides; a third of the congregation sitting with their backs to the speakers. Perhaps there is no building in our town so heavily built. The timber is massive, and its appearance will give us some index to the character of Burrillville forests a hundred years ago.

CHAPTER IV
Old Places

On the margin of Round Pond in Buck Hill Woods is a cave where a nest of counterfeiters once worked. They called the place Newport when they talked with each other before strangers. It was only a new port on the shores of the round frog pond. The members of the gang lived in the region now called Burrillville and in the adjacent towns. Silver money was rare then. They made old Eighty-six and Spanish milled dollars. The cavity in the rock that led to their den was hidden behind the trunk of a large rock birch and covered by a flat stone. Parts of the forge and a pile of cinders were lately to be seen there. The aperture where the smoke came out was about thirty feet from the door.

They made two sorts, plated and mixed. The plated were easily tested. If suspected, a knife soon cut through the thin silver coat and revealed the copper on the amalgam. One of the gang went one evening to a hotel at Brandy Hill. He became very tipsy and having the ready in his possession, he lavished it freely and spent several silver dollars in treats. The large crowd stared. Where did he get so much specie? The thriving farmers around could hardly find enough to pay their taxes with, and how could the idling swaggerer be so flush? The rumor of a swindling game gained credence. The barkeeper looked at the dollars and found them all of the same date. The man was arrested and when charged with the crime, confessed it. Several of his confederates were taken and brought before a justice at Chepachet. The cave was searched. The tools were found and produced in the court room. The old "bogus" was produced and the chief of the gang brought forward for examination. He was cool and cunning and evaded the questions.

Critical mechanics had examined the modus-operandi of the counterfeiting apparatus, and it was suggested to the court that the key that pressed the die must be struck fairly and squarely or one side of the coin would be thicker than the other. The court would know whether the chief was an expert or not. The ordeal was known only to a few who were conducting the prosecution. The prisoner could only see the game by his quick shrewd musing, when the hammer was put into his hand. The dies were placed in the " bogus," the prisoner was asked to strike the key, and the adroit schemer did strike a blow that, to use his own language as he told it afterwards, "brought the dollar clean to an edge on one side."

Some were satisfied that the bungling specimen before them was the work of an innocent man. But others knew the craft of the chief, and the examination went on. Soon a witness said that one of his neighbors who was a clothier, had promised his cloth screw to the counterfeiters. This clothier was son-in-law to the justice. He looked around the court room and saw sympathy for the prisoners, for already many of the first families for miles around had been implicated. The rigor of the questioning was abated and the accused soon discharged. In later years, common report linked one and another with the plot, but no legal process was used to bring them to justice. The visions of wealth grew dim that had lured men from the path of honest toil to secure ill-gotten gold—the bubble burst, and left them poorer than ever. A stain was upon their reputation for all their after lives.

Among the natural curiosities of this town, one of the most singular is a cave sometimes called, "Cooper's Den." It is located on the road leading from Glendale to the old Stephen Cooper house now occupied by John Paine. There is a high jagged ledge just in the verge of a wood. We remember ten years ago standing on the summit of this precipice with Calvin S. Keep, an old teacher of Burrillville. We dropped a stone while Calvin held his watch to see how many seconds it took for it to fall that he might thus calculate the distance. We have forgotten how far it was, but it is the highest rock in Burrillville.

A few days ago we went there again to explore the cave. Climbing half way up the cliff by clinging to the rocks and bushes, we found a narrow opening through which we crawled and soon found ourselves in an irregular room about 8 feet wide, 12 high and 30 in length. There are apertures where the light can enter. It looks as though the rocks had been violently cleft asunder by some tremendous subterranean convulsion. It was a fearful looking place. It was twilight when we entered, and the dim shadowy appearance made us shiver. We remembered the rumors we had heard of snakes. Our fancy made frightful forms of every jutting crag, and we were glad to emerge into sunlight. The rocks were so poised as to seem in momentary danger of falling. There is a tradition that here, too, silver money was coined. It was when all this region was forest, and the lonely cavern afforded a secure retreat to the company. No one would be likely to find them unless some hunter might chance to stumble upon them in pursuit of game that should run into this ledgey covert. The place is sometimes called "The Forger's Cave." Standing outside, the frowning rocks seem propped by the chestnut trees that lean against their sides. Large fragments appear to have been broken off by the frost and rolled down the hillside. Parties picking berries often come to this locality and merry shouts peal among the rocks. The broken echoes rustle down the valley startling the timid hare in the brake and causing the crows to make their way farther into the rocky wood.

On the farm of Smith Battey are found beautiful specimens of crystallized quartz. They are regular in form, and although not so dense as some diamonds, they will make a slight mark on glass. They are translucent, some of them are delicately tinged with purple hues, while a few of the smallest are yellow. Lapidaries find them too minute to work to advantage while they can get those of the same quality from the Old World in large blocks. Some of the jewelers of Providence obtain stones of the same sort at Bristol, R. I., which they set in gold rings. A few years ago, Dr. Chandler, Dentist, of Pawtucket, paid a visit to Burrillville and examined the diamonds on the Battey farm. He has made some experiments with them as a material for the manufacturer of mineral teeth. They worked well and he has already composed several complete sets.

In the same locality we found shining particles of earth resembling silver, which an analysis proves to be decomposed isinglass. A little to the northwest of Smith Battey's residence on his farm is a large rock upon which an excavation is to be seen which will hold several quarts. It is rumored that it was made by the Indians as a sort of mortar in which to pound corn. It is evidently artificial. The position makes it improbable that it could have been made by the action of water. Perhaps this was the red man's grist mill when the Nipmucs ruled lord of the ascendant in the forest of the Shining Brook.

In the valley of "Muddy Brook," about half a mile from its source was once a bark mill. Unlike the mills of our time, the bark was ground between stones and by horse power. One of these stones is now the curbstone of a well nearby. The mill was small, about a hundred hides a year being tanned, besides the woodchuck and squirrel skins that the boys prepared to make whip lashes and money purses. It is about thirty years since it was used and it gradually crumbled away, its moss grown roof fell in, and it assumed an aspect altogether interesting in the eyes of the antiquarians. A little below the bark mill is the site of the turning lathe of Shadrach Steere. Here were made spinning wheels, the pianoforte of our industrious grandmothers. Those solid oak highbacked chairs still to be found in the farmhouses of Burrillville and the adjoining towns were most made here. Heavy old men who would break down in the light fancy chair of modern times were safe in the old substantial seat of the quaker pattern. At last, hoe handles, scythe-nibs and bobbins were turned here. The little mill has rotted down, the dam is gone, and the speckled trout play undisturbed in the crannies of the pool where the old flume once stood.

A few moments at the "Old Paul Place" and we close our cursory glances at old places. Not far from the center of the town is a house, fast crumbling down, which has long been known by the above title. It was originally the residence of an ancient family of Ballous, a common name in this town. A little to the east of the old castle are four graves where they are buried. It was afterward occupied by Paul Smith. The old man met with many misfortunes which gives the place a romantic interest. His wife was insane for many years. She was confined in a lonely room and with none of the appliances with which modern science and philanthropy sooth and improve the stricken mind, she sank into hopeless idiocy. One of the sons, an athletic young man, was engaged in a foot race at Slatersville when he burst a blood vessel and died in a short time. Several families have resided there since Paul Smith died, but the edifice is at present forsaken. The moss-grown roof has partly fallen, the massive chimney is breaking down, and the wild wind shrieks through the crazy fabric like the pitiful wail of its ruined mistress. The forest is growing up all around it and people do not like to frequent the place after nightfall. The raven croaks hoarsely from the open gable, and the twilight bat flits undisturbed through the forsaken and desolate apartments.

CHAPTER V
Natural History

We are lovers of nature, and if we do not always look with a critical eye of scientific accuracy, we view with interest the animated creation that inhabit our woods and meadows. We hear the whip-poor-will wail out his plaintive story and see the night hawk wheel his circling flight. The bat is flitting his eccentric course through the twilight, the owl is shrieking out his discordant notes, or the wheatear is making shrill music with his rare scream.

Early dawn gives us the songs of the robin, the twitter of the lively wren, and the harsh scream of the beautiful jay. A few mornings ago, we saw a bald eagle sweep in lofty magnificent curves over Pascoag Pond and launch like an arrow of light through the sky far over the wild waste of Malavera woods. We have orioles and humming birds, and then we have animals of which we are not so fond.

The rattlesnakes are not all gone. The ledgey summit of Buck Hill can boast a few of these venomous reptiles. There is a point, on the north side of the road leading from Pascoag to Thompson where the cautious hunter does not like to venture at some seasons of the year. Occasionally one of these snakes may be seen hanging from the side of an old barn in that region where he has been nailed by the boys. We heard of one a few years ago that was kept alive for some months. He was brought to the village of Pascoag where he was looked upon at a safe distance by many. Those who did not know his clumsy habits thought him a dangerous thing to have at liberty. It could not glide rapidly like some snakes and its active keeper could watch its contortions and avoid its fangs while he left him to show all his natural motions. But most of our readers will agree with us that the deadly Crotalus ought not to be at large without having his poison teeth extracted.

Among the unique animals that we have seen in this town was a white rodent. It was caught by a brother of the author in a box-trap set upon the top of an old stone wall. It was a little smaller than our ordinary red squirrel, but resembled it in all other respects except its color. Its eyes were red and its fur as white as snow. We kept it in a cage for several months. It learned to turn a wheel and appeared as active as the red, black or gray variety. It was presented to a gentleman of Providence, and we have not heard of it since. Whether its hue changed as it grew older, whether it still attracts the curiosity of amateurs in natural history, or whether it has died in its loneliness, we are not able to inform our readers. But we assure them an animal more perfect in form and motion has never been seen in Burrillville. Black squirrels so numerous in the middle and western states are never seen in our woods. The gray variety are plenty.

Burrillville: As It Was and As It Is by Horace A. Keach 1856

CHAPTER VI
Glocester and Its Division

From 1636 to 1730 the territory which forms our town was included within the limits of Providence. In the latter year an act was passed by the General Assembly of His Majesty's Colony of Rhode Island "to incorporate the outlands of Providence into three towns." A Committee had been sent out by Roger Williams to survey the parts north of the city, and when they looked from Solitary Hill near Triptown over the barren lands, they returned and made their report that "no one would ever settle" beyond that point. But after the lapse of almost a century, there were inhabitants enough to warrant new towns, and Smithfield, Scituate, and Gloucester were formed; because "the prudential affairs of Providence had become heavy and burdensome."

The original town of Providence extended from Seekonk Plains to Douglas. The act of incorporation gave us the liberties and privileges of other towns of the State. The franchises and protection of the Charter were ours. We could elect our officers; we could send two deputies to the next General Assembly; we could send one grand and one petit juror to the superior courts; and we could have our proportion of the interest of the bank money appropriated to the use of the towns of this colony, according to the sums that the lands, lying in our town, were mortgaged for. The expense of surveys, roads over our rocky hills, money paid to the Indians, for the poor, of which there were more than at present, and the many burdensome taxes that oppressed the colony prior to the Declaration of Independence had compelled the town to mortgage their lands.

In 1806, Glocester was divided. Since the jurisdiction of Glocester extended over our territory for a period of seventy-six years, her archives must be searched that we may form proper ideas of the condition of public affairs at the time we commenced our corporate existence.

In 1798 the British currency was employed, and pounds, shillings and pence were the familiar terms of financial parlance. A little prior to this, corn seemed to be a standard of value, and we find the town treasury filled with it. December 10th, 1787, licenses were granted by the town council in these words: "To the six above named persons to keep a tavern in the house wherein he lives for one year from this time, provided they maintain good order and rule and pay into the town treasury each the sum affixed to their names, viz.: "No. 1, six bushels of corn; No. 2, four bushels," and so on. The corn was used for the support of the paupers. Persons were made poor by the poison extracted from corn, and when a citizen had been at expense for their maintenance, the council voted him a compensation in corn. A large part of the earlier council records consist of allowances of this kind.

    A little later we find a portion of the currency consisting of silver dollars. Some who had been dilatory in application for license were allowed to sell, "till the remainder of the year on the payment of three shillings." In 1791 from nine to eighteen shillings was the price of license. In 1800 the council voted that a special license be granted to——— on payment of fifty cents to sell spirituous liquors by the gill on Wednesday next. It does not appear what day Wednesday was, but we may presume that it was town meeting or training day. Neither is the result of the speculation recorded. The number of persons licensed the first year of this century was seventeen.

    In 1806 Glocester began to post her drunkards, but the same year licenses were given to twenty-six persons and they paid $75 into the Treasury as their contribution towards the support of the poor, with which the township *might* be burdened. Glocester at this date was twelve miles square. The people thought it too far to go to Chepachet to Town Meeting, so on the 17th August, 1805, it was voted, "That Messrs. Zebedee Hopkins, Seth Hunt, Abraham Winsor, Daniel Tourtelott, Bazaleal Paine, Joktan Putnam, and Edmund Waldron, be, and they hereby are appointed a Committee to draft a petition to the next General Assembly, to divide the town by the east and west line through the middle of the town, free from expense to said town, and signing the petition in behalf of said town.

    On the 16th April, 1806, they instructed their deputies "to use their utmost influence for a division of said town." The influence of the Deputies resulted in the passage of the following Act:

    An Act to divide the town of Gloucester, and to incorporate the north part thereof into a town by the name of Burrillville.

    Section 1. Be it enacted by the General Assembly, and by the authority thereof it is enacted, That the town of Gloucester, in the County of Providence, be divided into two towns, by a line drawn westerly through the middle of said town to the line of the State of Connecticut; and that the northern half of said town, thus divided and set off, be incorporated into a township by the name of Burrillville, and that the inhabitants thereof shall have and enjoy the like benefits, liberties, privileges and immunities, as the other towns in this State generally enjoy, and are entitled to.

    Section 2. And be it further enacted, That the freeman of said town shall, and may assemble in town meeting on the third

Monday in November, A. D. 1806, to elect their town officers, and transact all other business which by law a town meeting may transact; and that Simeon Steere, Esq., be authorized and directed to issue his warrant to any constable in the said town of Burrillville, to warn the freemen of said town to meet in town meeting for the purposes aforesaid, at such place, and at such time on said day as he may in his warrant appoint.

Section 3. And be it further enacted, That Messrs. Joshua Bicknell, Joseph Rice, and Thomas Mann, be, and they are hereby appointed a Committee to make an equal division of the poor, now supported at the expense of said town of Gloucester, between the two towns, and also of the debts due or owing, and money belonging to the town of Gloucester, and of the debts due from the said town, which said division shall be settled and made in proportion to the last tax assessed in said town.

Section 4. And be it further enacted, That said Committee be authorized and empowered to run the division line, after-described, to set up monuments and boundaries thereon, and to report to the General Assembly at the next session.

On the 17th October, 1806, the town of Gloucester *Voted*, That Jesse Tourtelott, Thomas Owen, Esq., and Col. Elijah Armstrong, be and are hereby appointed a Committee in behalf of the town of Gloucester, to attend the State Committee, to see to the division of the Poor, Taxes and Debts between the towns of Gloucester and Burrillville.

The following Report was submitted at the February Session, 1807: The subscribers being appointed a Committee by the Honorable General Assembly of the State of Rhode Island and Providence Plantations, at their October Session, AD 1806, to divide the town of Gloucester, in the County of Providence, did on the tenth day of November last, agreeable to our appointment, proceed to make the division as follows: Began at the southeasterly corner of said town, and measured the easterly line of said town to the south line of the Commonwealth of Massachusetts, which we found to be ten miles one-half and seventy rods; then began on said easterly line, five miles one quarter and thirty-five rods from said southeasterly corner, and there erected a monument, it being south eighty degrees, west twenty-three rods and eighteen links from the northwesterly corner of Benjamin Waterman's dwelling house; from thence we ran a course north eighty-six and a half degrees west, making monuments and marking trees, to the easterly line of the State of Connecticut, and there erected a large monument with stones: which course makes the dividing line between the towns of Gloucester and Burrillville.

We then proceeded to make an equitable division of the poor, supported at the expense of said town before said division between the two towns, and also of the debts due or owing, and money belonging to said town of Gloucester, and of the debts due from the said town, which said division we made in proportion to the last tax assessed in said town, which proportion is as five hundred and forty-eight dollars and seventeen cents, to one thousand dollars, for the town of Gloucester, and four hundred and fifty-one dollars and eighty-three cents for the town of Burrillville, of which division of said poor, and the debts due to and owing from said town, we made a particular statement and report, and lodged with the town clerks of each of the said towns. All of which is humbly submitted by your Committee.

JOSHUA BICKNELL
JOSEPH RICE,
THOMAS MANN.

April 20th, 1808, Gloucester Voted, "That Col. Elijah Armstrong and Jesse Tourtelott, Esq., be and are hereby appointed a Committee to settle all amounts, dues and demands which the town of Gloucester has against the town of Burrillville, and are hereby empowered to call on the town treasurer of the town of Burrillville, in order to close all amounts and demands existing between said towns.

The final legislation of Gloucester upon this subject was in 1809. At the August town meeting of this year it was Voted, "That the town of Gloucester be divided by a northerly and southerly line." This appears to have been done for Buncombe, as no action was ever taken upon this vote, which seems to be extending the jurisdiction of a town "to the fullest extent." But the inhabitants of Gloucester were always Democrats par excellence, and while the ruins of Acote's Fort frown over their capital, they will rather enlarge than lessen the right of the people.

CHAPTER VII
Modern Legislation

The old town retained the original name of Gloucester, and the new town was called Burrillville from the Hon. James Burrill who was the Attorney General of the State of Rhode Island. James Burrill was born in Providence, April 25th, 1772. He graduated at Brown University in 1788. Choosing the law for his profession, he began his legal studies immediately after leaving College, and was admitted to the bar before he attained his majority. A few years later he stood at the head of his profession in Rhode Island. By the General Assembly of 1797 and by the people for seventeen successive elections, he was chosen Attorney General.

The decay of his health and other causes induced him to resign that office in May, 1813. In 1816, he was appointed by the General Assembly Chief Justice of the Supreme Court, having been for several years previous Speaker of the House of Representatives of Rhode Island. The next year he was placed in the Senate of the United States, of which he remained an esteemed member until the period of his death, Dec. 25th, 1820.

On the 17th day of November, A. D. 1806, the freemen of Burrillville convened in town meeting for the first time. Capt. Joktan Putnam was chosen Moderator and Daniel Smith, Jr., was elected Town Clerk. At this meeting it was voted "That Capt. Joktan Putnam be a committee to attend on the town Clerk, to wait on the Hon. James Burrill, Esq., attorney general of the State of Rhode Island, to receive a set of books that he makes a present to said town." These books were to keep the records of the town in, and upon each one was this label: Presented to the town of Burrillville by JAMES BURRILL, Jr., Esq.: 1806.

The first Town Council consisted of the following persons: John Esten, Esq., Simeon Steere, Esq., Samuel Smith, Amaziah Harris, William Ross, Moab Paine, Levi Lapham.

The division of the town was a part of the business of this meeting. Daniel Smith, Esq., and Capt. J. Putnam were chosen "a committee to attend the Grand Committee in running the dividing line between the two towns, and also in settling the said town's business." The representatives to the General Assembly were then called *Deputies*. Capt. Pitts Smith and Capt. James Olney were elected for the February Session.

The next meeting was December 2d, 1806, fifteen days later. It was "for the special purpose of choosing a representative to the Tenth Congress." The meeting dissolved, then adjourned to the Hotel of John Wood, Esq., and it was declared to be "again in being." It was Voted "to do no business in Town Meeting after sunset." Again they met on the 14th of February, 1806, and adjourned to the 17th, at the Hotel of John Wood. At the meeting on the 17th, when the town had existed three months, and the lines had been established, it was Voted, "That the Charter of the town of Burrillville, and the Report of the State's Committee in the division of the two towns be lodged in the Town Clerk's office."

There had been manifested a disposition to avoid, or at least delay the payment of the Grand Committee, but at the annual meeting, April 15th, 1807, it was Voted "To provide some way to pay the Grand Committee." A highway tax of $1500 was ordered, and a poll tax of 75 cents. August 25th, 1807, the first money tax was imposed. It was only $500. The poll tax was 33 cents. The money tax was to be paid by the first of December or interest might be collected of the delinquents. the custom of the old town in regard to the poor was adopted, and they were sold to the lowest bidder. This year they sold for $200.

The town meeting was sold next. June 6, 1808, it was voted "That the next August town meeting be at Russel Aldrich's upon these conditions: that he pay to the town treasurer the sum of $16.25, within one week after said meeting, to which condition said Aldrich agrees, and also voted that said Russel Aldrich have privilege to prosecute any other persons for selling liquors on that day and place." The above is a literal transcript of the record.

Here was the first Maine Law in Burrillville. Law might be invoked to defend an impolitic monopoly, but may not be used today to protect the liberties of the citizens. We shall see how law was again employed in the cause of temperance forty years later. It was sold again in September, 1808, with a recommend to the town council to grant the bidder a license on the meeting days. This year it was bought for $23.00. In 1810, it was $50.00. This year the town council was sold at auction as appears by the following vote. "Voted that the privileges of having town council set at their houses one year, be set up at public auction, and the highest bidder to be the purchaser."

In 1812 it was voted that the soldiers drafted in this town receive four dollars per month premium above the eight dollars they receive from the United States. The State quota was 9300 men and in 1814 Burrillville voted to pay thirty dollars to each man drafted in this town. In 1819 it became apparent that the sale of the town meeting was a nuisance. It had been carried over to the west side of Buck

Hill, and the residents of the eastern district had to travel a dozen miles and along a miserable driftway over the mountain. It had been sold at the Jirah Ballou place, and the people of the west side swore in their turn. A committee was appointed "to confer with the Societies of the Baptist meeting house to gain their approbation to have the town meetings held at the old meeting house for the future."

From the record of 19th April 1820, it would seem that office seekers were less scrupulous than the "fierce democracie" wished them to be. It was voted "that from and after this date, no man shall be elected to office in said town who shall give any valuable consideration therefor."

When in 1825 an epidemic raged in the town of Douglas and Uxbridge in Massachusetts, which was supposed to be the small pox, there were a few instances of the disorder in this town. The council order that "the lands leading from Dr. Enoch Thayer's to Mr. Asa Burlingame's be fenced up at the east side of the road that leads from Uxbridge and intersects with said road, and also the same road that leads eastward to the Providence and Douglas turnpike road to be fenced up at the said pike road, so people shall not travel said road between the two fences without permission of the said council, owners excepted." "Also voted that Dr. Thayer's house be considered as a hospital for the said disorder and all persons are prohibited from frequenting it without said permission under penalty of the law." The road leading by John White's to Enoch Thayer's, thence by Peleg Young's was also to be fenced. Dr. Levi Eddy was appointed assistant superintendent of said hospital. This legislation seemed to be based upon the principle that the health of the people is the supreme law.

In 1834, there were many complaints for injuries received at bridges for want of railing. They were not in the excellent condition in which we find them now.

In 1844 it was discovered that the line dividing us from Gloucester was not properly established. On motion of Eddy Keach, Esq., a committee was appointed by the General Assembly to examine the survey. They reported that Gloucester had one thousand and forty-nine acres more than her proportion of the territory. The report was accepted and a committee was appointed who ran the line anew and the above tract was added to our domain. There is no doubt in the minds of Rhode Island men that the State line should have extended three miles farther to the north. This would have given our town a valuable region now belonging to the towns of Douglas and Uxbridge. The controversy between this State and Massachusetts about our northern boundary was finally terminated by a decision of the U. S. Supreme Court in favor of Massachusetts.

In 1839 the question of license came up. There were 101 for granting "Indulgences" and 49 against it. In 1844 it was voted "That no strong drink be brought into the meeting house yard." Stands and booths had before this been built around the Town House, and the activity of the sales was patent upon the common in front where rings were formed around drunken rowdies, who were pummeling each other with a will.

In 1848 the sale of rum in the adjacent woods was made a penal offense. At a later date the town seemed unanimous against the licensed sale of rum. No licenses are at present granted. The temperance reform has been of untold value to the town of Burrillville. Despite the curses of demagogues, the influence that has prevailed in favor of sobriety has added much to the security of property among us, guarded many young men from the dangers of dissipation, flung its protection over many a home, and those noble souls who made Burrillville the banner town and will keep her where she is are deserving the gratitude of all who love our best social interest.

We know that the evil skulks around at twilight and in the woods, but the bold notoriety that characterized it in 1840 will never return. We once had twenty-two violent deaths in ten years to be traced directly to intemperance. We will now protect ourselves. We love, we reverence, the blessings and privileges of the fireside, and we fling defiance at the ruffian crew who have determined to invade them. The scorn of all good men shall be upon them while the shafts of truth fall thick and fact into their discomfited ranks. The true man's eyes will see the brand of Cain on the brow of one who shall, in 1856, deal poison to the inhabitants of Burrillville.

Our town this year completes its first half century. On the 17th of November, 1856, will be the fiftieth anniversary of our first town meeting. How few will vote for President this autumn, who voted for Thomas Jefferson or John Adams in 1801. Most of those whose recollections are linked with the 18th century are gone where the turmoil of political controversy will agitate them no more.

CHAPTER VIII
Old Men

Within the memory of our elderly men there were open fields between Mapleville and Solomon Smith's. It is now thickly wooded. There was once an old barn at the brook in the woods. It was used to store the produce of the meadows that then stretched through the valley.

The Harrington house was a little way west of the Smiths. The old family burying ground is still pointed out by the road side just in the edge of the forest. The family of Harringtons was very large and they were a very thirsty set. One of their customs was to tap a barrel of cider on its arrival home and drink it all up before it was unloaded from the cart. A part of them died there and the rest moved away. Rufus Smith's grandfather could discern that when he went by there "the air smelled sweeter."

The old house near Martin Smith's was occupied by this family. It has been lately torn down and moved away to Buck Hill. There are none of the name left. Seventy years ago there was a Physician by the name of Harrington. He lived in the Smithville district. Dr. Bellows, so long a resident in the Colwell neighborhood, was one of his students. Dr. H. was one of the great men of the bygone generation.

We will briefly refer to one or two other men who will be remembered by some who are now living. Joktan Putnam was one of the old inhabitants of Rhodesville. Mr. P. was a great pursy man, fond of public employment, rather dictatorial in his manners, and a lover of good drink. He was for many years one of the assessors of taxes, and when men came to him to complain of the high rates, he said, to use his own phrase, he "always riz the taxes and soon got rid of the complaints." He was chosen the moderator of the first town meeting in Burrillville held Nov. 17, 1806. When they were nearly 70 years of age, he ran a race with Noah Arnold, and Joktan beat. So vigorous was the old age of our early settlers. He was the owner of the plains at Harrisville and a tract in Herring Pond wood, still called Putnam Pasture. In his political preferences he is believed to have been a tory. He became involved in debt in his old age and bartered his premises at Rhodesville for wild land in the town of Sutton, Vermont. The land in the above State is still occupied by the

Burrillville: As It Was and As It Is by Horace A. Keach 1856

heirs of Joseph Putnam and Charles Taft, once a resident of Burrillville.

Another of the old school was William Rhodes. When a boy, he was poor. He learned the trade of a cooper and went to the West India Isles to work. In his frequent voyages, he learned the art of Navigation, and engaging in the more lucrative occupation of a Privateer intercepted many English vessels on their way to the West Indies laden with sugar and molasses. He covered the wharves at Providence with his cargoes, and at one time felt so rich he "didn't care for John Brown, Clark and Nightingale, nor the d—l."

He sold his prizes for continental money, and his wife urged him to invest it in real estate, but he refused. It became almost worthless. Capt. R. said it was the only time he thought his wife knew more than he did. He bought at Harrisville, then called Rhodesville, built the large house on the corner, and owned the Othniel Young farm, the Smith Wood farm, and much land beside. He used to ride to the city on horseback. He often took a trip to South Carolina where he owned a store. As a mark of his activity, they tell of his standing upon a stick of timber thirty feet long and going the length of it at three hops. There are many of our old people who well remember Capt. William Rhodes.

Every Spring, regular as the singing birds, a lone man walks through this town. For forty years he has made his annual tour, sometimes coming several times in a season. We hear of him at a distance. He goes to Unadilla in New York upon his circuit. For many years he came with the same dress, a wine colored suit. Tradition says this was to have been his wedding costume, but he was disappointed and the most marked habit of his sad life was the care with which he cherished this suit. He would enter a house and sit a long time musing, pensively and silently, never speaking unless questioned, living in a world apart, unmindful of all the present, his spellbound memory was wandering back through the vista of shadowy years, to the halcyon days of his prime of life. He would ask for thread and from what was offered him he would select the color of his wedding suit, and then proceed carefully and patiently to darn the threadbare places, and he thus at last acquired the name of "The Darned Man."

The children know him the country round, and he is seldom rudely treated by them. His visits among us will soon be over, for he is now an old man. The blighted genius, for he had talent, the true lover, the melancholy worshiper among the ruins of a broken altar, will soon go home. After the fitful fever of a lovelorn life, he will rest in Elysium.

CHAPTER IX
Internal Improvements

We have 103 miles of road. Our highways are of all grades and run to and from all points of the compass. A few years ago our most excruciating route was over Buck Hill. But after a series of complaints and the payment of much money for damages done there, the town voted to repair it, and we have now no better road in all our borders. It is so steep, however, that it will need constant watching or the rains will ruin it.

We have 14 miles of stage road. A coach runs daily from Pascoag to Chepachet enroute for Providence. Another leaves Pascoag every morning to meet the cars at Waterford. These are all the facilities for travel at present.

The Woonsocket Union, alias the "Air Line," runs nine miles in this town. This road was surveyed in 1853. In March, 1854, the Railroad Commissioners went over the land and made awards to the several land owners. Work was commenced, and after a large expenditure, the hands were dismissed and the shanties sold at auction. The work is at present at a dead standstill.

The "Woonasquatucket" will extend about 10 miles in Burrillville. It will run alongside Wallum Lake and that section, which is thickly wooded, will receive much pecuniary benefit. The beauty of that romantic water will be appreciated by those who will ride through Douglas Woods to the music of the "steam calliope." We quote the following from a Patriot of last winter. Its paternity has been attributed to "Horace."

No stranger who visits the town of Burrillville fails to note the dearth of all comfortable means of locomotion. Now, in mid winter, it is true we have the glibbest sort of sleighing, but this is for the *elite*, for our pleasure seekers. But those who are abroad on business find their loads upsetting, our merchants fail to get their goods in due time, and our manufacturers wait for their coal. We have no Railroad. No locomotive ever startled echoes in our valleys, and our people must plod long miles before they can take the cars. Our older men can remember when the only conveyances were the lumbering coaches on the Providence and Douglas Turnpike. Lowing herds now range along its deserted sections; and sheep nibble the grass that grows within the ruts. Five hundred feet above the level of the sea, we could not even have a canal. Those who would see how it looked out of the woods, must go over the breakneck road across Absalone Hill, and when they greeted sunrise on its topmost summit, they saw the city of Providence at a distance that demanded three hours of hard travel.

Farmers cut wood and dragged it with slow pacing oxen to the city. They converted it into coal and carted it twenty-five miles. Many who lustily cried their "char c-o-a-l" along the city streets early in the morning had been driving all night. They said "it was a black, dirty business, but it brought clean money." After a while "McKenzie's stage" began to run from Pascoag to Providence. Mac had served eight years apprenticeship on the Hartford Turnpike and he thought he could endure the roads of Burrillville. Early and late, in shine and storm, mid snow and sleet, all weathers, all hours, he drew the rein and cracked the whip, —the indomitable Mac! He was a clever driver and it was cheaper to ride with him than to go on foot. His muscular form seemed to bid defiance to the elements; in the cold of January and in the sultriness of July, he brought us the daily mail. When the muddy turnpike kept him back, we could hear his shout in the darkness and the muffled step of his tired horses. But Burrillville highways were too much even for him. He went to California where he still plays the Jehu among the gulches, through the valleys, and along the rugged passes of their quartz hills.

We think we need the railroad. Our farmers could then readily avail themselves of the markets of Woonsocket and Providence. Our manufacturers could easily reach Boston or New York. Our thinkers find themselves in rapport with the last steamer at Halifax, and the last speaker at Washington. Our Sunday Schools go on excursions to Rocky Point, and our invalids breathe the salubrious air of Newport. In summer, botanists from the city would pluck flowers in our fields; in winter orators from the city delight audiences in our halls. Sportsmen would come out here. We have trout in our brooks, rabbits and partridges in our groves, foxes and rattlesnakes, too, among our ledges!

The "Woonasquatucket" has just asked the General Assembly for a charter. This road, too, will hit Burrillville. Two railways! What will become of our interests? It was predicted by some conservatives that we should be injured by the factories. But half a million is now invested in our mills and our town has steadily advanced in all the elements of prosperity., Neat, thriving villages, and a happy population of villagers, attest the value of the loom in Burrillville. And it will be so with the Railroad.

I am told that there has been enough subscribed to the Air Line to grade it to Pascoag. There is now due from subscribers about $100,000. This would enable the contractor to go right ahead with it. The best judges of the value of such property give it as their opinion that when completed, the stock will be among the best in the market, if not the best. Not till the Pacific Road is done and the auriferous hills of Oregon, the Sandwich Isles, and the treasures of the Eastern Indies make its freight, shall we ever see such a road. The chief city of New England will, by the Air Line, be linked with the largest city in America. With a straight line and a double track, they may defy all competition. Who will tempt the Sound around Point Judith and through Hurl Gate when he might by the "lightning train" land in the Empire city sooner? Give us the Air Line. Those who sell wood and those who buy flour, those who sell cattle and those who buy hay, those who sell books and those who buy papers, those who spin cotton, weave shirts, forge axes, plate hoes, or whittle axe-helves; those who want to get to the city in the winter and those who would escape to the country in the summer, will all thank the enterprise that shall build the Air Line.

Burrillville: As It Was and As It Is by Horace A. Keach 1856

CHAPTER X
Education

    The author can remember when some of our schools were kept in dwelling houses. Most of the school houses were in a dilapidated condition. They were sure to be set where several roads met. The internal arrangements made them unfit for school purposes. Some of the scholars faced the wall, some were roasted by their proximity to the stove, while little martyrs hung with their heels dangling above the floor. No means were provided for ventilation, and if the cool air whistled in some old cranny in the crazy fabric, it was to chill and endanger those who were nearest to it.
    It seldom entered the heads of the inmates that this rude structure was made to study in, and so they mused of mischief and meditated mutiny. The examination of the schoolmaster was made by a sporting survey of his physical proportions, and if he happened to be of athletic size, dubious shrugs telegraphed it round the hall of science on the first day of school. To be a good boxer was a qualification as important for a teacher in those days as it is for a Congressman now. I am not sure that the manners of some of our members at the Capitol are not the result of interest taken in school or college mutinies. To thwart the master's wishes, to impose some clever trick upon him and escape detection, or to rebel against his authority and fling him out of the school house, these were deeds that met the applause of the majority of the scholars and not a few of the parents.
    But changes took place gradually. Better school houses were built, and these were located in some retired place a little back from the highway. The prejudice that those encountered who advocated the policy of progress manifested itself in many ways. Men grumbled about their taxes, they tried to outvote those who wanted better houses, they had got all their "larning" in the old house and it was good enough for anybody's children. In this way the fogies talked themselves hoarse.
    But the most singular mode of opposition to a good edifice was manifested at Mapleville. The new school house, now the old lecture room, was just completed. It had never been occupied. One morning the passerby found the windows all smashed in, not a pane of glass unbroken. A club with which the insolent deed was done

was found nearby. The criminal was never discovered. The District met to repair the ruin. They drew several loads of dirt around the house to cover the broken glass and purchased new windows. No interference with the building ever took place afterwards. It is standing now and is used during this Presidential campaign as a Rocky Mountain Cabin.

When the Hon. Henry Barnard was elected to the office of School Commissioner for Rhode Island, he paid several visits to this town. To him we owe the Manton Library, the neat school houses that beautify Burrillville, and the deeper interest we all take in the culture of the young. To his labors we are indebted for the noble position our schools assume today.

When the new school law went into operation, the districts were remodeled and new boundaries established. There had been much complaint about the boundaries, and the first school Committee consisting of Messrs. Nelson Smith, Joshua W. Ballou, Lyman Copeland, Asa Paine, Francis H. Inman and David P. Harriman were assailed with numerous petitions for a revision of the districts.

In November, 1846, the town voted to instruct the committee in relation to this revision, and the 14th of the same month, the committee met to take their instructions into consideration and embodied them in the following vote, which was passed by the committee: "That the lines forming the boundaries of the sixteen districts of this town, be so amended as to include the *home farms* of all houses now included in said districts." Thus the law remained till the spring of 1856. During the controversy in district No. 7, (Harrisville) this vote was much discussed. The school committee met at the house of Isaac Steere on the 10th of March, 1856, and taking up the old law, "voted, that the same be and hereby is annulled." They then "voted, that the home farms appertaining to any dwelling shall be taxable in the district within the boundary lines of which such dwelling house may stand."

Again May 6, 1856, the school committee tried their hand upon this question of boundaries of districts with the following result: "Voted so to amend the action of the last meeting in regard to the taxation of home farms as to read as follows:" "Voted, that the home farms which shall actually be such at the time of assessment of any tax shall be taxable in the districts to which the dwelling connected with the said farms shall belong."

There has been but one printed report of the school committee. A report has been presented annually, but Burrillville has no printing press, and we are an economical people. The report of 1847 penned by Francis H. Inman Esq., was printed by order of the town. The motion was made by Solomon Smith, Esq., who was "afraid we should never have another so good, for one important member of the committee was about to remove from the State." The printing was done by Col. S. S. Foss at Woonsocket. This is the nearest press. It is ten miles from the center of Burrillville.

The Committee prepared a set of rules, had fifty copies printed, and a copy was posted in each school room in the town. These have furnished a standard of schoolroom manners. The neat aspect of the modern rooms has nurtured respect for the place and improved the conduct of the pupils. But the great influences that have produced refinement in the deportment of our students have been the employment of female teachers, and the introduction of music as a relief to the tedium of constant study. The rude young man who would resist the will of a master will cheerfully comply with the commands of a smiling schoolmarm. It has been suggested by some who have the reputation of our national assemblies at heart, that it would be well to send a few strong minded women to Washington to hold the balance of power in the American Senate. The suggestion will be seriously thought upon.

The committee of 1847 introduced a uniform set of school books. This lessened the labors of the teacher and it was better for the scholar. They established a depot for the sale of suitable books in town. Three sessions of a teacher's institute were held and the ideas imparted have exerted a beneficial effect upon the schools of our town.

Our school rooms have neat desks, the walls are adorned with maps and diagrams, and the teacher's desk is filled with a good assortment of apparatus. The great want is a school district library and we hope the suggestion of our present commissioner will be carried out by the General Assembly and our schools in common with those of the State be furnished with good libraries.

There is but one public library at present in the town. At Pascoag is the "Manton Library." It contains about nine hundred volumes. Here our citizens can find standard history and romance, travels and choice biography. The traveler who sojourns with us through the sultry summer may find his favorite volume upon its shelves. Our young people may cultivate a taste for reading that shall chasten and refine their life. In mature years when "the fever of the world" is on them, they will fling by the carking cares of material interest, and as they bask in the genial light of literature exclaim with the sainted Channing, "God be thanked for books."

In 1823 the farmers about the little hamlet of Smithville collected a library of three hundred volumes. Rufus Smith, Esq., was the first librarian. For awhile it was kept at his hotel which was the old red house in the corner of the roads near the Tar Kiln Saw Mill. It was afterward kept at the Smith Academy and finally removed to the dwelling of Coomer Smith, Esq., who for many years had it in charge. In 1845 it was divided, and the shareholders took the books to their homes. There is now no public library anywhere in that neighborhood.

The following final decision of a case arising under the School Act will be of interest to the inhabitants of Burrillville. It was in the case of Joseph O. Clarke v. school district No. 7. A Corporation may bind itself by a negotiable promissory note or bill of exchange for any debt contracted in the course of its legitimate business; that is, in any matter which is not foreign to the purposes of its creation.

A school district (a corporation under the School Act) gave its promissory note for monies hired to discharge debts incurred in the building of a school house and otherwise: Held, that in so doing it was contracting debts in a manner foreign to the purpose of its creation; and that the provision of the School Act, giving this class of corporations power to raise money by taxation, cannot be construed to forbid a borrowing of money for a legitimate purpose. 3. Rhode Island Reports 199.

CHAPTER XI
Temperance

The habits of inebriation that prevailed during the Revolution were disseminated through our State. The people who dwelt in the territory which is now Burrillville became slaves to the popular custom. The settlers who endured the privations of life in the forest resorted to the rum cask for the stimulus that should nerve them for their daily labors and dangers.

There was scarce a dwelling in which "the drink" was not to be found. The woodman laid the brandy bottle in his cabin, and the mower took his glass of West India at the end of each swath. At all elections, voters were jolly at the expense of the candidates. On all festive occasions convivial mirth grew rude as the glass went freely round. He who did not drink was a churlish Puritan. The child in the nurses' arms sipped the sugared lees of the glass its father had drained. At weddings the bride and groom were pledged in a full bumper. At funerals the guests expected to enjoy the good cheer that shortened the days of the neighbor they buried. Foaming tankards of brown October enlivened the winter evenings. He who went to the house of a friend thought himself insulted if he was not asked to drink.

Whether men heard of a death by intemperance or by lightning, it was with similar emotions. They saw no way of averting the fatal necessity. The credence of the many had called alcohol a luxury, and the coincidence between faith and practice was complete. That reform had not yet been inaugurated that has since gladdened so many homes and lighted beacons to guide the young past the breakers of dissipation.

An occasional warning would be given, but the true remedy was not seen. The clergyman who should have pointed out the woes of the drunkard's life was himself a victim. The teacher who should have guided his pupils along the sunny path of healthful Temperance was whelmed in the maelstrom of excess. The press that has since scattered so many facts, God's handwriting against iniquity, was then silent or the medium of Anacreon's songs in praise of wine or the songs of modern poets who have wreathed their laurels around the brow of Bachus.

But a better day was dawning. The generous voices that

spoke for the drunkard had an echo in Burrillville. When that reform began that has been linked with the name of Washington, there were few in our "outland" town to speak in its favor. But strangers came to help us. Reformed drunkards told us their story and we crowded the old school houses to hear them. Then we talked the matter over in the barrooms and at the corner of the streets and at the singing school and the quilting. We differed in opinion. Some thought it was all a speculation. Some saw their silver shrined goddess in danger and shouted lustily against the movement. But we all loved to hear the reformers sing, so we went in great crowds to every meeting and concluded if they could do the miracle they told us of, we would let them try their hand on some of the rosy-faced topers of our town.

When the "Honest Quaker" made his pilgrimage to our town, we had nine public and popular places for the sale of poison. This was in 1844. The village of Harrisville had two hotels. This village seemed to be the center of the movement. There were but a few factory villages in our town then, and Harrisville was a convenient rendezvous for the friends of reform. It was in the heart of Burrillville, and it became the residence of several powerful advocates of progress. Meetings were held there each Sunday evening.

There were gatherings at four places beside. At Pascoag, Eagle Peak, Mapleville, and the Bee Hive, lectures were given in regular alternation. A special omnibus ran to convey the speakers and a choir of singers. Old men and matrons, young men and maidens, came to the meetings. There were no serious scruples against the employment of the Sabbath for such a purpose. We are not a bigoted people.

There was a freedom of speech that made the movement popular. Our choir was half the audience. When they sung "Old Burgundy" or "Clear the Track," young men kept time with their boots and old men thrummed it upon the seats as they had beat the "devil's tattoo" on bar room benches. If the mood of the speaker demanded a pensive song, the sweet "Long Ago" of Gough was sung, and the spell of its tender words lingered long in the memory of our artless peasantry.

Among the prominent speakers was Dr. Christopher C. Harrington. He was young, talented, ambitious, and liberal. He began the work of temperance conference meetings and temperance debates. With a good memory, a fluent utterance, a caustic wit, and a bold, fearless elocution, he was well fitted to sway the sympathies of an audience. The ire of the friends of rum was awakened. It became apparent that the craft was in danger. Several of the lecturers were good looking men, and the women were frequenting all the lectures. The town votes "No License" with only a solitary vote for the indulgence. Something must be done. How to get rid of the Doctor was the question. It would not do to oppose him openly, that would only provoke his terrible invective and make him more popular.

A conspiracy was formed to use the language of one of the conspirators, "to blow him out of the village." A prosecution was instituted against him on a charge of larceny. The warrant alleged the stealing of *three cents worth of hay and twenty cents worth of grain* from the barn of Benjamin Mowry, Jr., where the Doctor was boarding his horse at the time.

The trial took place in Mowry's Hall and was one of the most exciting ever held in Burrillville. Christopher Robinson, Esq., of Woonsocket, appeared for the government and John P. Knowles, Esq., of Providence, for the defense. Each side had its partisans. The Temperance party saw the reputation of their champion at issue, and the opposition knew if he escaped he would be more sarcastic and effective than ever. Mere politicians looked on with interest for they saw the destiny of the new party involved in the result.

More than a score of witnesses were examined; the lawyers made elaborate speeches; the Court took time to deliberate, and the conclusion was a verdict of acquittal. The Temperance men rallied around their leader who, through all the trial had maintained the utmost nonchalance, smiling scornfully upon the array against him. They congratulated him upon his complete vindication of his character and invited him to lecture in their respective districts. The crowd dispersed. The tipplers went to drink, their smothered rage scarce allowing them to swallow. So ended the second experiment to invoke the aid of law in the Temperance question.

There was another lecturer who was not so fortunate in the maintenance of a character among us. Philander Brown, or as he called himself, Harvey P. Brown, paid us a visit. He was a tall, good-looking man with a plausible manner, a good voice, eloquent thoughts and words, and he made many friends, some of whom will not soon forget him. He lectured in many localities in our town and did good, but his influence was neutralized by the "confidence" game that he played upon some of our citizens. After a residence here of several months, he left, several hundred dollars in debt. Mr. Brown has been unfortunate and, perhaps like many whom we liberally curse, he was more entitled to our charitable pity.

He was of an ardent temperament and in his prime he married the woman of his choice and settled in central New York. They had one child, a daughter, and their home bliss seemed complete. But the generous man had bitter enemies. His efforts for reform were opposed and his Eden of happiness assailed. His heartless opponents saw there they could most surely ruin him. They trumped up a charge of theft against his wife. Circumstances had been skillfully arranged, suborned witnesses warped their stories to favor her guilt, and she was convicted. When the verdict was announced, the impulsive Harvey rushed from the court room with his hands clasped on his burning brow, his reason with all its "sweet bells jangled" and his best memories wandering in the labyrinth of delirium. For many months he was a raving maniac. Then he left the scene of his brief joys and the next news he friends had of him he was in the town of Burrillville.

When he left Rhode Island he went to his old dome. He met his daughter, now grown almost a woman, but maddened again by the recollections that clustered around the hearthstone where he saw his heart's best idol shivered, he turned away and is now wandering among strangers, the creature of circumstances, the ruined plaything of demon despots.

Lecturers sometimes came from Woonsocket to speak at the White School House, formerly Smith's Academy. The town became the "banner town" in the temperance work. The nine rum shops were closed. None was sold except clandestinely. "No license" was voted for several successive years prior to the passage of the "Maine Law." The bar room of one of the prominent hotels was transformed into a reading room.

At last the Maine Law was enacted. The first case under it was the State vs. A. F. Harris tried Dec. 22, 1853. It was doing a good work when the decision of Justice Curtis in the Circuit Court checked it. Dealers were emboldened and the friends of prohibition were disheartened. A reckless gang came from Woonsocket Falls and opened a rum shop, brothel, and gambling house at a place called Round Top. They defied law. They were just upon the line and could run into Massachusetts as a last resort. They talked as border ruffians always talk. We were sorry when we heard the plaint of wives and mothers in that part of the town. Fifteen warrants were issued and the guilty parties were sent to the Court of Common Pleas. But the late *or* and *and* decision has declared those warrants void and the rude bachanalians are more defiant than ever.

Perhaps this may be as good a place as any to mention a singular outrage that took place here last fall, since some have hinted that it might have some relation to those trials. The author who was educated for the bar had a law office in the village of Harrisville in the center of Burrillville. There had been no lawyer located in Burrillville for thirty years. Our office was the basement of a wooden block built by Smith Wood for a hotel. In the eve of the 5th November, 1855, we left as usual and went to our boarding place. The next morning we found it had been entered, our library destroyed, and papers, the result of four years of industry, stolen. The library had been selected with care. It consisted of the best modern text books and upon the shelves adjoining was a good collation of literary works, which were mostly untouched.

The books seemed to be laid open by a knife running through

the back. The leaves were cut and carved as though the spirit of a demi-demon nerved the Vandal hand that did it. A large proportion of the books were carried to the verge of a wood nearby and strewn along the road. Among the papers was a personal journal of five year's date giving a sketch of rambles in New England, Canada and New York during vacations. There were many letters and papers of library value. No trace of the perpetrators of this deed has yet been found.

If the malicious act was inspired by hatred of our words on acts of reforms, we know that the thanks of some ready to perish are ours. No embarrassment we have suffered makes us willing to forego independence of thought or action. We have as many books as ever and can say with Prospero, "My library is dukedom large enough."

We find in our scrap book under date of March 20, 1855, the following words, "There are reasons why Burrillville should interdict the sale of intoxicating liquors which will apply as well to most parts of Rhode Island. We have a large manufacturing interest. To carry on most of the processes in the factory, sober men are indispensable. The unsteady hand, the besotted mind, the reckless temper, produced by alcohol, would be fruitful of evil results; machinery would become disordered: work would be neglected; the hands would disregard the wishes of a tipsy overseer and confusion would reign over all the establishment.

Our manufacturers have usually been in favor of laws to keep rum from their workmen. Many of them have interdicted liquors among their employees. They were no doubt incited to this by views of interest. But it proves as useful to the servant as to the master. The diligence and frugality caused by temperate habits is a good thing for all parties. We have among us a large class of foreigners who are imbued with the principles of Catholicism; they have no lofty sentiments to restrain them from gross indulgence—the majority of them are unable to read. As guardians of the public weal may we not demand the enforcement of the Maine Law;—surely the ignorance and brutality of this class renders it dangerous to allow them the stimulus of gin. They have always been kept poor at home by their intemperance. The smoke of the distillery has blackened the beauty of the finest of lands. Famine has stalked across her borders. Pestilence has sent thousands of imbruted peasants to the grave. Philanthropy has somewhat mitigated the evil, but the labors of Father Matthew and his coadjutors were but partial. Avarice will still murder its victims and law must interpose. The distiller and dram seller must not be allowed to live by the misfortune of other."

We commend to the lover of humanity the following words of a generous Reformer. The author is Geo. S. Burleigh, Esq., of New York. Many of our readers will remember Charles Burleigh, a lecturer upon Freedom. He has often spoken at Pascoag and Mapleville. The orator and the poet are brothers. The article is entitled "The Wreckers."

The Wreckers
by George S. Burleigh

Hark to the roar of the surges!
Hark to the wild wind's howl!
See the black cloud that the hurricane urges,
Bend like a maniac's scowl!
Full on the sunken ledges
Leaps the devoted barque,
And the loud waves, like a hundred sledges,
Smite to the doomed mark.

Shrilly the shriek of the seamen
Cleaves like a dart through the roar;
Harsh as the pitiless laugh of a demon
Rattles the pebbled shore!
Ho! for the life-boat, Brothers!
Now may the hearts of the brave,
Hurling their lives to the rescue of others,
Conquer the stormy wave.

Shame, for Humanity's treason;
Shame to the form we wear;
Blush, at the temple of pity and reason
Turned to a robber's lair;
Worse than the horrible breakers,
Worse than the shattering storm,
See, the rough-handed remorseless Wreckers,
Stripping the clay yet warm.

Plucking at Girlhood's tresses
Tangled with gems and gold;
Snatching love-tokens from Manhood's caresses,
Clenched with a dying hold.
What of the shrieks of despairing?
What of the last faint gasp?
Robbers, who lived would but lessen your sharing
Gold, 'twas a god in your grasp?

Boys in their sunny brown beauty,
Men in their rugged bronze;
Women whose wail might have taught wolves duty,
Died on the merciless stones.

Burrillville: As It Was and As It Is by Horace A. Keach 1856

Tenderly slid o'er the plundered,
Shrouds from the white-capped surge;
Loud on the traitors the mad ocean thundered,
Low o'er the lost sang a dirge.

Wo! there are deadlier breakers,
Billows that burn as they roll,
Flank'd by a legion of cruel Wreckers,—
Wreckers of body and soul.
Traitors to God and Humanity;
Circes that hold in their urns
Blood dripping Murder and hopeless Insanity,
Folly and Famine by turns.

Created with wine redly flashing,
Swollen with liquid fire.
How the strong ruin comes, fearfully dashing,
High as the soul walks, and higher.
Manhood and Virtue and Beauty,
Hope and the sunny-haired Bliss,
With the diviner white Angel of Duty,
Sink in the burning abyss.

What if the soul of the Drunkard
Shrivel in quenchless flame!
What if his children by beggary conquered,
Plunge into rain and shame;
Gold has come in to the Wreckers,
Murder has taken her prize,—
Gold, though a million hearts burst on the breakers,
Smothers the crime and the cries.

CHAPTER XII
Freedom

There are many friends of the slave among us. Slavery once existed in the territory that is now Burrillville. In 1728, two years before the town of Glocester was incorporated, the General Assembly of the colonies enacted:

"That if any child or servant shall refuse to obey the lawful command of parent or master, they shall be sent to the House of Correction till they have humbled themselves to their parents or masters satisfaction, and if any children or servants shall presume to assault or strike their parents or masters, they shall be whipped at the discretion of some justice, not to exceed ten lashes."

No slave could be manumitted till the master had given "a bond of not less than one hundred pounds to indemnify from all charge for or about such slave in case he or she by sickness, laziness or otherwise be rendered incapable of maintaining themselves."

In 1714, sixteen years before the town of Glocester was formed, the colony made the following Fugitive Slave Law. It rendered it the legal duty of the early settlers among these hills to arrest and secure any slave that might escape and travel this way, and if there were any who would not "conquer their prejudices" and return the flying bondmen, the emissaries of King George II who ruled here then would hasten to show their devotion to their master's interest by calling them to an account. Here is the law.

An Act to prevent slaves from running away from their masters, etc.

"Whereas, several Negro and Mulatto Slaves have ran away from their masters and mistresses, under pretense of being employed in their service, and have been transported out of this Colony, and suffered to pass through several towns under the aforesaid pretense, to the great damage and charge of their owners and many times to the loss of their slave.

Be it therefore enacted by the General Assembly and by the authority of the same: That no ferryman or boatman whatsoever within this Colony, shall carry, convey or transport any slave or slaves as aforesaid over any ferry or out of the Colony without a certificate under the hand of their respective masters or mistresses or some person in Commission of the Peace, on the penalty of twenty shillings to be forfeited to and for the use of the Colony, to be recovered upon conviction thereof before any two assistants or Justices of the Peace of such town where such offense shall be committed, and shall pay all costs and charges that shall arise on his or their carrying or transporting any slave or slaves as aforesaid to the owner thereof, if not exceeding forty shillings, before any two Justices of the Peace, and if above forty shillings at the General Court of Trials, by action of trespass on the case. And all his Majesty's Ministers of Justice and all other his subjects in this colony, knowing of any slave or slaves traveling through the township where they dwell without a certificate as aforesaid are hereby required to cause such slave or slaves to be taken up, examined and secured so as the owners of such slave or slaves may be notified thereof and have their slave or slaves again, paying the reasonable charges arising thereon."

The above is a law that was in operation when Burrillville was comprised within the limits of the town of Providence. From "broken chronicles of senility" we learn that Slavery once existed in this town. The land on the northwest of Herring Pond was cleared by the labor of twenty colored men, who were owned by a Mr. Brown of Providence city. John Inman the first, as he is now called by the only man who remembers having seen him, was the owner of a slave.

Moses Cooper, who was a contemporary of John Inman had a slave. He was called Jack. He ran away, and his master heard nothing of him for several years. He made inquiries at great distances, but was one day surprised with the news that his cunning servant was living in the State of Massachusetts only a few miles from his old master.

Mr. Cooper mounted his horse and went to reclaim his property. He brought him home and told him he would cut his throat if he ever attempted to escape again. Jack lived with him for the rest of his life. Deacon Salsbury, who has frequently been referred to in these pages, tells us he has worked with him for many a day. The boys, sons of Mr. Cooper, used to lay all the bad mowing to Jack. The old man heard all their charges and then said he believed "Jack did most all the mowing." Upon Oak Hill on the farm now owned by Jason Olney, Esq., two rough stones mark a spot still known as "Jack's Grave." Here rests the last serf of Burrillville.

We have among us some who are advocates of Woman's Rights. Lucy Stone has been here. She lectured to large crowds at Pascoag and Mapleville, and a number of copies of the "Lily" are taken.

One word about Spiritualism and we close our notice of Reforms in Burrillville. There have been a few circles in our town. The orthodox think it the work of the Devil. The free-thinker at first called it Magnetism, then Odylic Force, then didn't know but it might be Spirits. Those who imagined it the result of sleight o'hand or legerdemain are giving up that idea, and a few calm, cool questioners are quietly asking for "Light, more light."

The existence of supernal beings has always been a cherished faith among the dwellers in rural towns. Fairies dance in our meadow, Naiads rule our brooks and rills, and "Wood Nymphs decked with daisies trim," preside in our groves. And until we can forget the gossip by the winter fireside and the witching tales of Walter Scott, we shall lend a willing ear to the messages of angels.

CHAPTER XIII
Religion

Perfect freedom of conscience is the especial birthright of every Rhode Islander. The religious sentiments are left untrammeled and their free action gives them a vigorous and healthful strength. In Burrillville, half a dozen sects are struggling for influence—if not for supremacy. In our remarks about these sects, we will first refer to the mission of Elder John Colby.

This remarkable man who readily won the confidence of all classes of the community, made frequent and long visits to this town in its infancy. He was a native of New Hampshire and traveled and preached in many of the States for a term of nine years. His zeal knew no bounds. His first visit to Burrillville was upon the 10th of Oct., 1812, and on the same evening we find him preaching, although he had traveled from Providence over the roughest of roads.

The eloquence of Whitfield or the apostolic energy of Wesley could not have had more influence over the rustic inhabitants than did the fervid utterance of the devoted Colby. There was no portion of the town that did not enjoy the privilege of listening to him. "In season and out of season" he labored everywhere. The old people among us will remember when he preached at the Old Meeting House, in the hall of Capt. Wm. Rhodes, the hall of Esquire Wood, in school houses in various localities, and at the dwellings of Esquire Steere, Solomon Smith, Mr. Barnes, Mr. King, Andrew Bullard, Asa Burlingame, Mr. Salsbury, Esquire Cook, Jeremiah Mowry, George Brown, Mr. Gleason, Daniel Smith, Mr. Thayer, Esquire Arnold, and in all the adjoining towns.

The people almost idolized him. Worn with his excessive labors, his friends saw the seal of death set upon his pale brow, and upon his visit to Burrillville, Jan. 1st, 1817, they persuaded him to rest for a season. He found them sedulous to minister to his comfort, and deeply anxious to bring back the boon of health. But his work was done. He made his home at Simeon Smith's, Deacon Salsbury's and Capt. Rhodes' for several weeks, but growing no better he went to Providence to consult with Dr. Gano, Pastor of the First Baptist Church in that city skilled in diseases of the body as well as maladies

Burrillville: As It Was and As It Is by Horace A. Keach 1856

of the mind. By his advice he traveled toward the South, but while on his route to Charleston, S. C., where he intended to tarry a while, that if possible the balmy air of those mild latitudes might improve his lungs, he was arrested at Norfolk, Va., by the mandate of death. Here "the silver cord was loosed, the golden bowl was broken," and the spirit of the sainted Colby left its frail tenement of pain and winged its flight to that better land where his affections had so long been placed. His body rests in the family burying ground of Wm. M. Fauquier at Norfolk, nine hundred and fifty miles from his childhood's home.

The First Freewill Baptist Church in Rhode Island is in Burrillville. It was gathered by Elder John Colby. The reformation commenced in Oct., 1812, and gradually spread through the town, then the residence of farmers only.

The Church was formed on the 15th of December, 1812. At its organization there were but nine members. They agreed to take the Scriptures of Truth for their guide "because" says their compact, "there is no one in our day wise enough to revise the laws of God or alter them for the better." The first church meeting was held Feb. 11, 1813. The first Freewill Baptist Quarterly Meeting in the State of Rhode Island was commenced at the Old Burrillville Meeting House on the 12th of March, 1814.

After the departure of Colby, Elder Charles Bowles of New Hampshire, a colored man, preached a good while in this vicinity. He was a man of talent and honorable mention is made of him in the life of John Colby. The people afterwards listened to Elder George Lamb, Elder Joseph White and Elder Zacharia Jordan of Maine. Still later Elder Bullock and Elder Jonathan Woodman were here. These filled the time until 1820, when Clarisa Danforth of Wethersfield, Vt., came among them. She was a woman of large gifts and immense crowds gathered to hear her. Through her labors the church that had been embodied eight years before was strengthened and enlarged.

Elder Reuben Allen, now of North Scituate, R. I., came here in 1821 and ever since that time he has preached often in different parts of the town. At the present day he is called upon to attend the funerals of many old people who having admired him in his prime expressed a desire that the gray-haired pastor might perform for them the last earthly service of faithful friendship. Among the occasional visitors were Elder John Burrell, of Parsonsfield, Me., Elder David Marks, Elder Richard Lee, of Springfield, Vt., Elder Ebenezer Searles of N. H., Elder David Sweet and Elder Crossman.

There were several preachers raised up in this church about thirty years ago. Elder Daniel Williams now of Killingly, Conn., Elder Smith Fairfield now in Maine, Elder Jacob Darling now in New

Burrillville: As It Was and As It Is by Horace A. Keach 1856

York, and two brothers, Abel and Adin Aldrich, now in York State, were of this church and began their ministry in this town. Elder Willard Fuller and Elder Joseph Walling labored here for several years prior to 1832. In 1836 the Pascoag Baptist Society was incorporated, and at the June Session of 1839 the charter was revived. A church edifice was erected at the village of Pascoag and dedicated Oct. 2, 1839. Elders Oatley, Cheney, Branch, and Allen were present.

Elder Augustus Durfee was ordained the first regular Pastor on the 16th March, 1842. It was about this time that the delusion of Millerism swept over the land. The Church at Pascoag met the fate of so many others, it was rent and torn by schism and weakened by the withdrawal of a portion of its members to worship in a school house nearby.

Elder Durfee asked for a dismissal. It was granted him and he went to become the leader of the Second Advent band. One member committed suicide by cutting her throat, and her zeal for herself and friends, on the near approach, as she believed of the consummation of sublunary things, was conceded to be the fatal cause. Many eyes were gazing at evening on the western sky, where nightly a brilliant comet spread its fiery trail far along the horizon. To some it portended the dissolution of the "great globe itself," while others calmly saw the strange visitant wheel through the visible portion of his eccentric orbit, obedient to the impulse of an invariable law.

Elder David P. Harriman of New Hampshire took charge of the church in 1843 and continued about three years to preach and teach a select school. D. H. Lord was the Pastor for two years, then M. H. Davidson one year, and then Elder Harriman was called here again and remained nine years. Elder H. was a man of liberal education and much of the time he was engaged in teaching. He was chairman of the School Committee during his resident here. The church is at present under the supervision of Rev. Mr. Weeks, formerly Professor of Elocution in the New Hampton Biblical Institute.

The Baptists have often worshiped in the eastern part of the town. For many years a Church meeting was held in the Esten neighborhood because it was so far to the Pascoag meeting. The Smith Academy was used by the Baptists for many years. It was the liberality of Nicholas Brown, Esq., of Providence, that induced the building of this structure in its present form. This generous man made donations to many districts in the State to enable them to add another story to their school rooms for the purposes of religious worship. He gave the glass and nails, the cash articles, for the White School House.

It was dedicated on the 29th October, 1823. It was a great

day for that little hamlet. They had struggled hard to produce that state of society that would warrant a regular meeting, and the house was crowded to perform the initiatory service. Prayer was offered by Rev. Mr. Westcott. The sermon was preached by Rev. Reuben Allen. About ten years ago the high pulpit and narrow galleries seemed to form so great a contrast with the modern buildings it was resolved to refit it. The desk was torn away, the two stories were separated, and now the upper room is a very comfortable place for meetings and social lectures while the lower makes a neat school room. When the friends of progress were battling against intemperance, here was the rendezvous for reformers in this vicinity. Some of the best temperance meetings in town have been held there when Johnson and Bell spoke, Sadler sang, and a large cold water band applauded.

When the first settlements were begun in the region of Pascoag, and for many years afterwards, the state of society was, to use the expression of an old settler, "rather heathenish." Among the first clergymen was Elder Bowen. His church consisted of only six members, but the old man was regular in his ministrations and labored many years in promulgating the truth as he believed it.

About forty years ago the "new lights" began to shine in the northern part of our town. A spirit of earnestness and fiery zeal was then shaking the Churches of New England and the movement has ever since been referred to as "the reformation." Elder Britt, a follower of John Wesley, was at that time preaching in Douglas and Burrillville. The fervid enthusiasm and "free and full salvation" of the reformers attracted a goodly number to their standard. The meeting house upon the plains now called the old Douglas Meeting House was built. Many of the first families on the borders of the two towns were represented in their congregations. The late venerable Moab Paine was one of their first converts, and for forty years was an exhorter among them.

Classes, the primary organization of Methodism, have existed among us through all the half century of our existence as a town. Whatever changes of form it may have undergone, the vital spirit and substance of Methodism has been present. The leaven has been ever at work. Sometimes the light has looked faint and dim. The haze of worldliness has enveloped it until it was well nigh useless as a beacon to the inquiring soul, but again it brightened and flashed its hopeful radiance into the gloom of despairing souls.

More than twenty years ago meetings were held at the "Huntsville Emporium." This had formerly been occupied for a store. It formed a plain, comfortable lecture room, and the good spirit glowed as gratefully in the hearts of those who worshiped there as among those who bowed around gilded altars and chanted their anthems beneath the Gothic arches of a grand cathedral.

In 1847 a church was organized. It was called the

"Methodist Episcopal Church of Laurel Hill." Aided by the liberal donations of George W. Marsh, Esq., a neat Chapel was erected and dedicated in 1848. The sermon at the dedication was preached by Rev. Charles Macready of the New England Conference. The Rev. ―― Cowen, a local preacher of the M. E. Church, officiated here for the first year after the organization. Since that date, the following appointments have been made by the Providence Conference:

    April 1848, Rev. James Weeks, resident, 1 year
    April 1849, Rev. Geo. Burnham, resident, 2 years
    April 1851, Rev. G. W. Wooding, resident, 2 years
    April 1853, Rev. E. A. Lyon, resident, 2 years
    April 1855, Rev. Chas. Hammond, resident, 1 year

Their present Pastor is Rev. Samuel Fox. When Mr. Wooding closed his labors, the members of the Church were 56, on probation 70. During the administration of Mr. Lyon, there was quite a revival. During Mr. Hammond's mission was a season of embarrassment and depression. Their Pastor was of feeble health, some of the mills in the vicinity had suspended operations, and a number of their working members removed to other villages. At the close of the Conference year, the members in Church were 62, with 23 on probation.

    The Methodists have a neat chapel. It is beautifully located. There are few more pleasant landscapes in Burrillville than a view from this point of the placid valley through which Clear River sends its line of light. Like "the changing spirit's rise and fall" in the experience of the individual Christian, the Society at Laurel Hill has had its variable history. Long may that small band endure and the victor's palm reward their self-denying labors.

    Until 1851 the people of Burrillville had never seen the solemn and impressive service of the Church of England. In the Spring of that year, the Rev. J. H. Eames commenced religious services at Mapleville according to the rites of the Protestant Church. These meetings were continued for two years and were well attended. For nearly two years, Mr. E. was making the tour of Europe and wandering among the ruins of Egypt and the Holy Land. The meetings were discontinued during his absence, but on his return in the Autumn of 1854, he recommenced services at Harrisville, and soon after removed to the Old Meeting House where they are regularly held at present. Sunday Schools and Bible Classes have been connected with all the services.

    Upon Mr. Eames' return from the East, he published an account of his travels in a neat volume and shortly after, his accomplished wife, who had accompanied him, gave us another. These were read with interest by their parishioners, and in connection with several courses of lectures upon the same topics, constitute the most liberal tribute that has yet been made to the intellectual and aesthetic tastes of our people.

In the neighborhood of the Old Meeting House are a large number of families who have listened to the Anglican service in the mother country. They gather upon the Sabbath day and listen with reverent attention to the services by which their religious affections were guided in their dear old English Homes.

About 1786 the Quakers began to hold stated meetings in Burrillville. They met at the house now occupied by Smith Battey. This place is in a pleasant valley through which flows a little rill called Muddy Brook. Notwithstanding its unpromising name, this stream is remarkable for the crystal transparency and purity of its waters. In a humble low-roofed cottage that adorned its banks, the little band of silent worshipers held their sittings. At the end of five years enough had been attracted to their assemblies to make the place of meeting too strait for them, and a comfortable house was built at the junction of three roads, upon a spot now included in the suburbs of Mapleville. The house is, like all their temples, a plain structure, two stories high, with unpainted seats, no ornament in the interior, and only a modest brown coat upon the exterior.

Here for nearly three score and ten years a little company have met twice in each week, except when the Monthly Meeting called them to Smithfield or Northbridge. They go to the latter places to their Quarterly Meetings and in the midsummer of each year, they go to Newport, upon Rhode Island, to meet with Friends from all parts of New England and the Union, and often to hear strangers from foreign lands. The example of the Friends exerts a healthful influence upon the moral tone of the town. Industrious and temperate, quiet and tolerant, helping their neighbors and doing good to their enemies, they furnish a daily tribute to the value of their peaceful faith.

There is no church of the Universalists in Burrillville, but many of our must influential men are of this faith. Rev. Mr. Fish of Hopedale has made occasional visits to the eastern part of the town, and the Rev. Adin Ballou, founder of the Hopedale Community of Restorationists has sometimes preached at the Town House. The Quarterly Meeting has been held at the Old Burrillville Meeting House.

There are but few gatherings of Universalists here now. They warmly welcome those who bring "glad tidings of great joy," but our isolated position renders it difficult for them to reach us from the city, and we are left destitute of the Gospel of the last and best Evangel of "Good will to man."

There are many who forty years ago would no sooner tolerate a believer in Universal Good than give the right hand of fellowship to a Musselman or a Hindoo, but the tendency of the visits of Ballou and Borden has been to make this class more liberal, and

Burrillville: As It Was and As It Is by Horace A. Keach 1856

now a minister of this denomination will call together a larger congregation than one of any other man.

CHAPTER XIV
Nature

If picturesque natural scenery has an influence upon the sentiment of veneration, we might expect to find in the vicinity of Allum Lake the home of those pleasing superstitions that humanize and refine the hearts of a simple peasantry. If one would hear gossips tell of ghosts or find men digging for silver at midnight guided by the magical movements of Divining Rods, or be pointed to haunted houses where troubled spirits "revisit the pale glimpses of the moon," let him frequent the rustic neighborhood of western Burrillville.

The impressions of those who dwell here are such as are made by nature where the untrained luxuriance of the primitive forest is ever in view. When they look from the summit at the northern end of the lake, they view a range of blue hills running along the western horizon as far as the eye can go and all nearer them is one wide expanse of heavy forest. The distant hills are a range that reach across New England. They run toward the north through Massachusetts, join the Green Mountains and beyond the 45 degree descent to the table land of Stanstead Plain.

At their feet Wallum Lake lies embowered in the grand old woods whose monarch oaks sent their roots down to its springs twice five hundred years ago, and whose giant arms today limn their mighty shadows upon the crystal mirror of its placid surface. Shall we go down to the bathing beach? Where the grape vines have woven their dense canopy over the witch hazel and from the larch to the maple across the bright bower made by the fantastic clusters of the twisted laurel—here is a place for the swimmers to disrobe. Newport nor Hampton Beach can boast such a boudoir. Step out to the water's edge. The whitest sand, the gentlest slope, no surf to startle the timid, or stones to stumble the careless. Can our swimmer's beach be beat?

Before the pale faces came to swim in these limpid waves did the aboriginal models of Apollo Belvidere pace these sands, and with the sturdy strength of their symmetrical limbs, go straight across the lake to yonder distant point. It might be done despite the distance. A white man did it once. It was a swimming race. A boat went alongside the swimmers and long ere they reached the shore one of them was taken in. The other pushed on, each stroke growing shorter and feebler until the panting victor struck his palm upon the sand beach and fell back into the water. His comrades rescued him, and years after Caleb used to tell the story of which he was the hard working hero.

Wallum Lake is noted for the purity of its water. The stream that rises here is called "Clear" river. Like the Mississippi until it unites with the Missouri, this river is clear until below the Laurel Ridge it receives the muddy contents of the Pascoag. When we go out in a boat upon the lake, we may see the bottom at twenty feet. The lilies whose white petals beautify the surface of several of our ponds are not found here for there are no muddy coves in which they could grow.

One of the coves is called "Deep Cove." In one place it is ninety-five feet deep. It was sounded by Samuel White, Esq., who has basketed many a noble fish from this lake. Another is called "Long Cove." It goes far inland running under a bold shore, where the shadows rest at sunset while the arrows of evening light are lodged in the bright tree tops of the opposite shore. Another is "Grassy Cove," and beside these is many a little nook and inlet where the fisher moors his boat and pleasure parties anchor for their lunch.

David Wilkinson used to say "if he was ever going to be drowned," he should want to be drowned in "Wallum Pond." This water has by some been called "Alum Pond" and they justify the name by referring to its superior clearness.

A few years ago there was a controversy between the Mill Owners on the Blackstone and the Blackstone Canal Company in relation to the water of this Lake. The factory men complained that the Canal Company carried the water around their mills. The Company claimed a prescription in the ponds from whence the water emanated, and among the original fountains was Wallum Lake. Pending the controversy, commissioners were sent to survey the Lake and note the rise and fall of the water through each month in the year.

The Manufacturers replied to the Company's claim that since they had done nothing at the Lake to raise the water above its natural level, they had no exclusive right to its use. The matter was compromised before it came to a final decision. Our Rhode Island manufacturers will never again be plagued by Canal Companies.

Clear river flows through Saxon Vale, where a neat village smiles along its margin, then past Graniteville it winds in beautiful curves through the village of Harrisville, the pine woods, along the base of North Hill, and between Mapleville and Oakland it unites with the Chepachet to form the Branch, the largest stream in Burrillville. There are seven factories on this stream. Upon its southern branch, the Pascoag, there are five mills within half a mile of each other. These factories have built up the largest village in our town. The Chepachet river has three mills in Burrillville. It is a small but durable stream. The Branch has three mills. This river conveys the water of all our brooks and rills into the Blackstone. Our rivers have been a source of great wealth. The building of a large reservoir is contemplated, which will double the water power of Burrillville.

There are many aspect of grandeur and beauty about our largest forest. From "Reed Swamp" to the Bay State line, from "Iron Mine Brook' to the "Wakefield Saw Mill," extending over six thousand acres. There is no other such "Boundless contiguity of shade" in Rhode Island. When we are upon the summit at the clearing near the Connecticut Line, we have the widest view in Burrillville. The neat farms of Thompson, the cozy village of Webster, the poplar rows on Brandy Hill and the distant forests of Woodstock are before us. A dozen spires are visible in our horizon.

Stand here at sunrise after a winter shower if you would view the most magnificent panorama that ever gladdened the dreariness of a New England December. The crystals of frozen spray in a myriad million glittering clusters burden every rood of foliage. The pine trees to their topmost twigs are bright with the frosty jewels. The flexible birch and young maple have yielded to the furious blast of midnight, and their pendant boughs are fettered to the snow crust among the elders and shrubby oaks. There is music for the ear as well as pictured beauty for the eye. Hark! up from the valley rushes the morning breeze and the clattering branches and creaking limbs give one continuous thunder of unwonted music. Aurora kisses the prisoned wood nymphs and flinging aside their pearls that descent in a radiant diamond shower, they wave their free scepters up toward the God of Day, as if grateful for their deliverance.

The effects of the terrible tornado of September 23, 1815, are still visible in Burrillville. We had large pine forests slightly rooted in a light soil and whole acres were laid prostrate. The hunter in our woods often stumbles over an old log half bedded in the ground and thickly covered with a deep green moss. When the farmers collect their fuel in the autumn, they break off the pitch-pine knots and during the long winter evenings, the big fireplace is ruddy with their glow and the women knit, the old men smoke, children play, and kittens purr around the cheerful light.

At the home of the author's childhood is an old apple tree which was blown down in that storm. A portion of the roots still clung to the soil, new shoots grew up from the prostrate trunk, and almost every year it has borne well. The highest portion of the old bole is scarce a yard from the ground, but this season it is as usual fully laden. If our reader will call at the "old Homestead" he shall be treated to Pomona's best from a tree that fell forty years ago.

If some of our readers have looked with cold and careless eyes upon the illustrated pages of Nature's book, and now smile with utilitarian incredulity at efforts to call men to love the beauty of our country, where "—Nature showed the last ascending footsteps of the God." Let us justify our mood by the following quotation from an eloquent and instructive author. After the cold winter scene above, a more genial picture from a southern pen will prove agreeable.

"Why, it was once said that the sky of Attica would make a Boeotian a poet; and we have seen even 'the red old hills of Georgia' draw inspiring melody from the heart of patriotic genius. Physical causes have always operated in the formation and fashioning of literature. In all the higher productions of mind, ancient and modern, we can easily recognize the influence of the climate and natural objects among which they were developed. The sunsets of Italy colored the songs of Tasso and Petrach; the vine-embowered fields of beautiful France are visible in all the pictures of Rosseau and La Martine; you may hear the solemn rustling of the Hartz Forest, and the shrill horn of the wild huntsman throughout the creations of Schiller and Goethe; the sweet streamlets and sunny lakes of England smile upon you from the graceful verses of Spencer and Wordsworth; and the mist-robed hills of Scotland loom out in magnificence through the pages of Ossian, and the loftier visions of Marmion and Waverly.

"I have stood down in Florida, beneath the overarching groves of magnolia, orange and myrtle, blending their fair flowers and voluptuous fragrance, and opening long vistas between their slender shafts to where the green waters of the Mexican Gulf lapsed upon the silver-sanded beach, flinging up their light spray into the crimson beams of the declining sun, and I have thought that for poetic beauty, for delicate inspiration, the scene was as sweet as ever wooed the eyes of a Grecian minstrel on the slopes of Parnassus or around the fountains of Castaly.

"Again: I have stood upon a lofty summit of the Alleghenies, among the splintered crags and vast gorges, where the eagle and the thunder make their home, and looked down upon an empire spread out in the long distance below. Far as the eye could reach, the broad forests swept away over the territories of unexampled productiveness and beauty. At intervals through the wide campaign, the domes and steeples of some fair town which had sprung up with magical suddenness among the trees, would come out to the eye, giving evidence of the presence of a busy, thriving population. Winding away through the center, too, like a great artery of life to the scene, I could behold a noble branch of the Ohio, bearing upon its bosom the already active commerce of the region, and linking that spot with a thousand others, similar in their condition and character. As I thus stood and thought of all that was being enacted in this glorious land of ours, and saw, in imagination, the stately centuries as they passed across the scene, diffusing wealth, prosperity and refinement, I could not but believe that it presented a nobler theatre, with sublimer accompaniments and inspirations, than ever rose upon the eye of a gazer from the summits of the Alps or the Appenines."

Burrillville: As It Was and As It Is by Horace A. Keach 1856

CHAPTER XV
Factories

In our notice of modern movements in Burrillville we will allude to the commencement of manufacturing. Forty years ago a simple hand machine was used to whip and pick cotton. It was a box about three feet square and one foot deep with ropes across it near the top on which the cotton was placed and beaten while the seed fell into the box below. The cotton gin of Richard Arkwright the humble baker of Bolton had not then come into vogue.

Solomon Smith was the architect of the first mill in Burrillville. It was built on the Tar Kiln River in 1810, 46 years ago. Thurber of Providence was the owner. The first wheel was a tub wheel which soon failed, then a bucket wheel was made which lasted thirty-three years. There was no gearing on the surface of the wheel, but it was on the shaft, so the usual strain was avoided. In later years the mill was run by Lewis Thompson. Thompson sold to Joseph Nichols who is the present owner. The mill is near the road leading from Mapleville to Woonsocket. Negro cloths are now manufactured there.

Rufus and Zadoch Smith built a factory on the same stream, a little higher up. Here were made the first satinetts in Burrillville. Some of the cloth sold for $2.50 per yard. Cotton cloth for pantaloons was then selling in Chepachet for 75 cents per yard, now sold for 14 cents.

The warps for the Smith factory were distributed about the neighborhood and woven by hand. Solomon Smith used to make the spring shuttle lathe, to weave by hand. An Englishman who used one of these said they would "never make looms to go by water for many men in England had undone themselves by it." But the "impossibility" has been done, the hand looms have vanished from our town, and the capital invested in mills of Burrillville is a standing rebuke to the incredulity of old fogyism.

The thriving neighborhood around the Smith Academy near where the first mill was located soon wished for a bank. Banks and factories are always built up together. They preferred a petition to the General Assembly and obtained a charter. The presidency was offered to John Slater, but he would not accept it unless the bank could be at his new factory village of Slatersville, and it was finally established there.

Another Charter was obtained, and this time it was located near the Eddy Cooper place. The vault was hewn from a solid rock, and the trap door that covered it could only be lifted by a tackle attached to the ceiling of the counting-room. If burglars had unlocked it, they could not have got at the coin unless they could have found the tackling. It was a safe bank.

Those who lived near the Smith Academy would not subscribe to the stock because they could not have it at their village. The old settlers assert that it might have done a good business there as there were many solid men in that vicinity. We will not stop to discuss the probabilities of its success under other circumstances or to speculate upon the causes or consequences of its embarrassment, but hasten to warn our readers not to receive the bills as they have been rejected at the Suffolk. *Mutatis mutandis*.

One of our neat factory villages is called Mapleville. The following notice of it appeared a few years since in one of the Providence journals.

"Mr. Editor: I will pen a word about the little village where I go to get the "Freeman." It is cozily nestled among the hills of northern Rhode Island. I can almost see the factory spire from the place where I now write. I remember when a school boy we used to play along the river there, then all forest. We would go up the stream to the beaver dam where the primitive denizens of that new region held undisturbed possession. The dull drumming of large wheels and the buzz of the whizzing spindle has scared them away. The woods have been leveled, but the grove still stands on some parts of the river's margin. The tall pine is left to wave in the summer winds and the hemlock with its perennial foliage gladdens the eye at all seasons, and the balmy breath of the maple still sweetens the air. That reminds me that I was to tell about Mapleville. I have left the village so often to saunter along a sheltered path through the grove that I was about to do so now.

We have one factory, this has made our village. All over this part of the State wherever there is a waterfall, a hamlet springs up like magic. On a little eminence overlooking the village stands an elegant Gothic cottage. This is the residence of the proprietor of the mill. Its low windows, large parlors, and the ambulatory promenade, its tasty fence, the trellised walk to the door, and the trees that surround it, evince the ability of the lord and the ideality of the lady.

We have one store where our Post office is kept. We have no tavern. We seldom see a man inebriated. Order and industry prevail. The rural scenery exerts a healthful influence on all. We have no gaming saloons to steal away the time of our young men. Our simple people pursue the even tenor of their way, avoiding the dissipation of cities and free from the cares of envious ambition.

We have one school. Here our little sprigs of humanity receive their inclination. A "school district library," such as they have in New York, is still a desideratum in this State. The cultivated tastes which might thus be formed would shield its possessor from coarse indulgences and give him the luxury of the most improving pleasures.

We have one meeting-house, for the "Friends" who worship here do not call their temples Churches. This unadorned structure reminds one of the times of Fox and Penn when simple hearted men rebuked the vices of the court and refused to participate in the crimes of the camp. The peaceful band that rallied around them has brightened a large page of modern history. Ever the advocates of peace and the truest friends of civil liberty and soul liberty, they often proved themselves real heroes by the fortitude with which they suffered for their principles. Now they are the friends of the slave and of the drunkard. They are the friends of education. We love to meet with them in that Quaint old meeting-house. We love to go there on a sunny Sunday morning to sit and muse with them. The serene quietude of their communion with Heaven hushes the passions to repose and chastens the too active pulse. The "still small voice" thrills the heart with its kindly monitions, and faith whispers resignation to our Father's will.

Sometimes they have preaching, and their chanting tone is burdened with real pathos. I am glad to know that the principles of toleration they have done so much to establish have imbued the people of Rhode Island with charity. When you become weary of the splendid ceremonial of your city churches, come out to the old Quaker meeting-house.

Mapleville! Isn't that a luscious name? It reminds me of rich lots of maple sugar which I used to get in Vermont. When you wish for a respite from the cares of the "sanctum," come out here and roam with me in the broad, free fields. With hearts attuned to nature's serenity, we will forget the ills of life and go tranquilly to our daily tasks.

I remain as ever. Yours hastily, "Horace"

CHAPTER XVI
The Present

Upon the preceding pages were hints about the state of various interests at the present time, but we shall attempt some farther sketch of things as they are. We, too, "shall cheerfully bear the reproach of having descended below the dignity of history if we can succeed in placing before the reader a true picture of the life of our people." When some future compiler of the history of Rhode Island shall seek from "scanty and dispersed materials" to portray the condition of his ancestors, some item from this cursory sketch may perchance subserve his purpose.

The climate of Burrillville is colder than that of Providence. We have more snow, partly the result of our altitude, and it may be partially occasioned by the larger amount of forest. The spring is about two weeks later than upon the shore south of the capital. Our coldest winds are from the southwest, but these are usually of short continuance. During the extremely cold winter of 1780-81, this wind was prevalent most of the time. It was impossible to keep the paths open and at last they were abandoned and the people traveled on snowshoes and drew their grist to the mill upon hand sleds.

The heaviest fall of snow we have had since 1800 was in the winter of 1836-37. The walls and fences were covered, and people went upon the hard crust across the fields without meeting with any obstruction for miles.

The heavy rains of the springtime do considerable damage in the lowlands. The most severe freshet for many years took place in the middle of the month of May, 1836. Several dams and bridges were swept away and deep channels were cut upon some of the intervals. But we are compensated by the enrichment of our natural meadows by alluvial deposits.

Our inhabitants grumble a good deal about our cold weather. Some of them imagine that a uniform temperature is the most conducive to health. This is a fallacy. Those who live in Florida feel a change of five degrees as sensibly as we feel a variation of thirty degrees. But these changes do not equally purify the air. The winds that whistle over our hills act as ventilators, and the change produced will do a thousandfold more good than harm. A lukewarm region is not as healthy as our own Rhode Island. True, without caution we are liable to the "pains and aches of rheumatism and the neuralgic twinges of "cold Sciatica." But there are more cases of rheumatism reported at Key West on the coast of Florida than on the New England coast. Persons sometimes find a relief from rheumatic affections by visiting a mild climate, but they are usually more affected than ever on their return. Some who never suffered in that way are victims after a residence at the South.

A good many of our citizens not having the fear of the Ague, dumb or shaking, before their eyes have gone to the West. When we see them return pale and thin, we feel content to breathe our native air although it may be frostier. Some are benefited by a western residence, but it is a doubtful experiment. If the reader will refer to that admirable work, "The Climate of the United States, 1842" by Samuel Forey, M. D. Surgeon U. S. Army, we will be content to dwell in Rhode Island.

There was formerly a great regularity in the seasons in this latitude. We had three successive summers cold and dry, then three wet and warm. Hay would be scarce the first cold season, still less the second, and upon the third only half the crop was gathered that would be realized in the wet seasons. One old farmer kept an account of a large meadow, and by counting the tumbles found from the last wet season to the last cold and dry one, a decrease of one-half.

About twenty years ago this rotation of seasons was broken in upon and now no regular rule can be found., One effect of the change has been a decrease of birds. Other causes may have contributed to this result, but several unusually cold winters and summers about twenty years ago is supposed to have kept away many kinds of birds. Night hawks were once so plenty that they were seen in flocks of hundreds like pigeons. They were often seen sweeping before a shower apparently striving to keep out of its way. We see a few now, but they are rare, and we can no longer find the amusement of our childhood in watching at twilight the eccentric gyrations and lofty flight of this singular bird. There were once a great many snipes in these parts. The moist ground of our numerous low meadows was their favorite resort. They are seldom seen now. March quails, once very plenty, are now rare. But the robin, the bluebird and the golden winged oriole still enliven our springs with their gushing melodies and cheer with their vocal joys our glorious midsummer days.

By the census of 1850, the number of inhabitants was 3538. Now they may be safely estimated at 4000. The larger part are employed upon the land. Our factories engage a great number. The various mechanical employments common in rural towns are well represented.

A more industrious people are nowhere to be found. The thin, hard character of our soil imposes upon our people the necessity of hard labor, and the prudent maxims of Poor Richard are a law to the daily conduct of our hardy yeomanry. In our variable climate, hay must be made "while the sun shines." The many cobblestones that must be picked up or made into wall to get them out of the way, causes a great deal of hard work. The large extent of land to be traveled over, the hilly nature of the surface, the many drains to be made, and the rough roads to be mended; these give little time for rest and none to waste.

The land in Burrillville is poor. Much of it is sand and gravel, sweet-fern hills and barren pine plains. There are many acres of interval land, furnishing only the poorest sort of bog hay. There are a few tracts in the valleys that might be made valuable by proper drainage. The culture of cranberries would give a better return than the poor swale hay mingled with checkerberry and foxglove. The value of land ranges from five dollars per acre on Buck Hill to fifteen hundred in the neighborhood of the factories. The effort to till too large an extent of land keeps our farmers poor.

We have few of the modern implements. The wooden plow is abandoned except for furrowing, and a few wheeled "Prouty and Mears" cut their even channels across our fields. But most farmers plow in shallow scratches as their fathers did, and following in the regular ancestral routine scrub over ten acres to glean the crops they should find on one. There is no Mowing Machine in Burrillville. We have a few Horse Rakes, and this is the greatest innovation upon the clumsy utensils of ancient date. We have a few Corn Shellers, and a Threshing Machine makes its autumnal perambulation through our town. The rude tools used by the farmers in the outskirts of Burrillville would excite smiles among the agricultural amateurs who are familiar with the advancement of the art near the metropolis.

It is said that in Belgium each three acres will support five persons. If the soil of Burrillville were fertile in the same degree, its territory would support more than fifty thousand persons, or nearly one third of the present population of the State. At its first survey, land in Burrillville was sold for 12 1/2 cents per acre.

Our town has 24 factories. They are scattered over several districts, from the edge of Douglas Woods to the Smithfield line. Manufacturing is now the leading material interest of Burrillville. When we remember that only half the power is yet occupied, we can hardly be too sanguine in regard to our future prosperity, nor need we doubt but the Air Line and the Woonasquatucket must be built.

The produce of the land that is not needed in the family is bartered at some of the stores for tea and coffee, ginger and raisins, calicoes and crockery. The frugal housewife takes her weekly stock of butter, eggs and cheese to the home market at the factory village, and the worthy matron feels commendable pride when she unpacks the proceeds before the large-eyed children at home. A bunch of raisins or a lump of sugar stills the crowing of the youngest, while a pair of shoes or a calico dress crowns the expectation of the eldest. There are dwellers among the hills on the borders of Wallum Lake who must go five miles to reach the nearest store. At Pascoag there are five stores within a mile.

Hoop poles, shingles and ship timber are prepared in our woods and carted a score of miles to market. The produce of the stone quarries is considerable. This is greater the year that a factory village is built than upon other years. A new village upon our streams is not the slow accretion of years, but it goes up all together. When our farmers go to the city, they often return with a goodly burden of groceries, which they find are cheaper there. If we have a railroad, it will bring the markets of Woonsocket and Providence near the common people of Burrillville.

Our clergymen labor with their own hands. There are many who do not like to hear a man preach unless he works. Some have preached here who were liberally educated, but often we listen to those who have no culture save that they can obtain in the intervals of regular labor.

Our young men who are desirous of a better education than our common schools afford, go to some foreign academy. The seminaries at Smithville and East Greenwich often have students from Burrillville. Our young ladies sometimes go to Providence or Warren for a few terms. The accomplished preceptress of the latter institution is a native of Burrillville, and parents love to confide their daughters to her charge.

Our homes are in a healthy region and we have the best of water. Those who reside in the villages are usually tenants of the owner of the factory, but the majority of those who live on farms own their homes. The buildings of Burrillville are not noted for their good proportions. There is scarcely a residence in this town that would attract the attention of an artist. Many of the houses were originally small, and successive additions have been made, more for convenience than show. The older houses were but a single story with a massive stone chimney in the center containing a large fireplace. It was once a custom to paint them red, and there are some now that blush for their own ugliness.

There is no provision made for ventilation in our habitations except the lowering of a window. Our sleeping rooms are the smallest in the house. The "parlor bedroom" is often no more than eight feet by ten. Bed curtains are retained by some, and while they mean to be hospitable, they almost smother the stranger in these unhealthy dormitories.

Some of the farmhouses have an outside door to the cellar so it can be entered without going into the house. Here is generally the dairy, though sometimes there is a separate milk house. In the cellar are stored the potatoes and other roots, our beef and pork, and cider. In our low chambers and garrets are stored the extra bedspreads and counterpanes and patchwork. The general use of stoves in our kitchens is shortening the lives of our citizens. A few wooden clocks, reaching from the floor to the ceiling, tick in solemn grandeur, while "the nicely sanded floor" is still an institution among us. Many of the windows of our farmhouses have panes of glass only six by eight without any blinds, while in the villages green blinds are oftener seen.

The floors of the best rooms are sometimes covered with "rag carpets," and here and there a parlor is furnished with a genuine "Brussels." A few of the first families are provided with "pianos" or "Melodeons" but many of our farmer's daughters hear only their own sweet voices or the songs of birds, except when a musical brother tunes a three stringed violin or makes strange discord with a broken-winded "accordeon."

Many of the parlors are furnished with a little recess used for a best cupboard to stow the "China," the blue crockery, and the shells that some rich uncle sent from the "Indies." The table is covered with the best books,—the old family Bible, Saint's Rest, "Life of Colby," and the "Young Man's Guide." The daguerreotypes of all their kinsfolks are dispersed among the books or ranged upon the mantel shelf.

Cheap statuary of plaster of Paris is placed over the fireplace, while around the walls are hung a few simple pictures, often representing scripture scenes, "David and Goliath," or "Christ Blessing Little Children; "Napoleon Crossing the Alps," or the "Portrait of George Washington," are often seen. Sometimes they have a sentimental case like "Burns and his Highland Mary." Where the daughters have been "away to school," the best room is adorned with their pen and crayon sketches and views of English landscapes with old castles, noble trees, or some grand scene upon the Hudson, give us pleasant and refining impressions. Some of the parlors are closed most of the time, being open only on Sunday evening, or for a party or a funeral.

In the yards of many of the farmhouses are fruit trees, cherries, pears and plums. There are good quantities of apples, and these are always before visitors. The farmer's company are invited when the weather is suitable to walk through the orchard and over the fields and meadows. Each man tells about his handy oxen and big pumpkins, his new ditch, or rotten potatoes, while the womenfolks are looking over the dairy and the garden, the bees and the poultry yard. Thus an autumn day goes by.

The barns of Burrillville are of all grades. Many of them are old and leaky, but those of modern date are better built, some of them being of the first class. Within a few years, basements are made to the barns. Some of the best kind are painted, have glass windows, and dome ventilators. During the summer of 1856 a moderate farmer in this town had his barn struck by lightning and consumed with his entire stock of hay and farming tools. We speak of it that we may allude to the liberty nature of our yeomanry. His friends collected several hundred dollars for his aid, his neighbors met and built him a new barn, and thus as a token of their regard for honest industry, they completely indemnified him for his loss.

The harsh winds make it necessary to build large sheds to shelter the cattle in the day time, and it is a large item of the farmer's expense to keep his buildings covered. Some of the best farmers have good wood houses, but many in the bye parts of the town have their wood pile in the open air. Some cut their wood no faster than they use it, and they would be obliged to stop in the morning to prepare fuel before they went to hoeing or mowing, if they could not leave it for the women folks to do. The cost of wood is but a trifle in some districts of Burrillville. In the forest of the western parts, large quantities are wasted every year. The market wood is culled out and the rest is left to rot. There is but little coal used here. Large quantities of charcoal are made, but it is sold in the city.

Many of the older sort of farm buildings are located away from the main road. A rough lane leads down to the house. Here is retirement. The rattling of wheels, the annoyance of peddlers, the dust of the highway,—they are secure from these. Here, with the woods all around them, they till the hardy soil, eat their coarse food with an appetite that the indolent epicure seldom brings to his perfumed viands, and sleep with a sweet soundness that kings might envy. The boys grow up tall and tough, the girls have natural waists, and a healthy color in their cheeks; all live without envy, and die without ambition, except to fulfill the duties of their humble but happy station.

In a great many circles that beautiful song is sung, entitled "The Dying Californian." Burrillville claims to be the birthplace of the authoress. Miss Catharine Harris of Pascoag composed the words, and they have been set to music by Mr. Taber of Providence. It is no wonder this is a favorite song. Who is there that has not some relative in the land of gold. "Some have a Sister, Some have a Brother, Some have a nearer one yet, and a dearer one than the other."

We give the lines as they were published in the *Morning Star*:

The New England Diadem gives its readers the following beautiful stanzas, which were suggested by hearing read an extract of a letter from Capt. Chase, giving an account of the sickness and death of his brother-in-law, Mr. Brown Owen, who died on his passage to California. We have but seldom met anything so painfully interesting, in every line, and it will be read with "teary eyes" by many who have lost brothers, fathers, husbands, or sons, on their way to, or after having reached, the land of Gold and of Graves:

> Lay up nearer, brother, nearer,
> For thy limbs are growing cold,
> And thy presence seemeth dearer,
> When thine arms around me fold;
> I am dying, brother, dying,
> Soon you'll miss me in your berth,
> For my form will soon be lying
> 'Neath the ocean's briny surf.
>
> Hearken to me, brother, hearken,
> I have something I would say,
> Ere the veil my vision darken,
> And I go from hence away;
> I am going, surely going,
> But my hopes in God are strong,
> I am willing, brother, knowing
> That He doeth nothing wrong.
>
> Tell my father when you greet him,
> That in death I prayed for him,
> Prayed that I may one day meet him,
> In a world that's free from sin;
> Tell my mother, (God assist her
> Now that she is growing old.)
> Tell her child would glad have kissed her,
> When his lips grew pale and cold.
>
> Listen, brother, catch each whisper,
> "Tis my wife I'd speak of now,
> Tell, oh! tell her, how I missed her,
> When the fever burned my brow;
> Tell her, brother, closely listen,
> Don't forget a single word,
> That in death my eyes did glisten,
> With the tears her mem'ry stirred.
>
> Tell her she must kiss my children,
> Like the kiss I last impressed,
> Hold them as when last I held them,
> Folded closely to my breast;
> Give them early to their Maker,
> Putting all her trust in God,
> And He never will forsake her,

For He's said so in his Word.

O my children! Heaven bless them!
They were all my life to me,
Would I could once more caress them,
Ere I sink beneath the sea;
'Twas for them I crossed the ocean,
What my hopes were I'll not tell,
But I've gained an orphan's portion,
Yet He doeth all things well.

Tell my sisters I remember
Every kindly parting word,
And my heart has been kept tender,
By the thoughts that mem'ry stirred;
Tell them I ne'er reacher the haven
Where I sought the "precious dust,"
But have gained a port called Heaven,
Where the gold will never rust.

Urge them to secure an entrance,
For they'll find their brother there;
Faith in Jesus, and repentance,
Will secure for each a share—
Hark! I hear my Saviour speaking,
"Tis, I know his voice so well,
When I'm gone, oh! don't be weeping,
Brother, here's my last farewell.

Having presented this tribute to the love of home joys in the hearts of my readers, I will revert to our domestic customs.

The people of Burrillville never know what it is to want for food. We have few among us who are rich, but we have none who are miserably poor. There are many whose daily earnings will only provide them with a livelihood, but these will always buy the best flour. The dainty luxuries that sometimes pamper the palates of the rich are seldom seen upon the tables of our farmers, but they have enough if it is coarse. Large quantities of beef and pork are used. No dinner can be made without pork or beef or mutton. We have good potatoes, beets, turnips, carrots, beans and peas, with all the esculents that the garden can afford. We know they are fresh and good. Our own hands gather them the same day they are eaten, and we do not have the poor withered and unwholesome vegetables that the common people in the city are often obliged to eat or go without.

We have one table staple which is a Rhode Island institution. We mean "Brown Bread." This is as much a Rhode Island invention as the "Rhode Island Greening." It is the best bread the world has ever produced. I do not mean the sort that is left at the doors of city tenements, but the real rye and Indian bread in bouncing great loaves, baked in a brick oven. Whoever has traveled in the Middle States will know how to prize this article. Unless he lives with a family from New England, he may travel for weeks and never see a slice of this staff of life.

We are so near the land of steady habits that we have fully adopted their grand Thanksgiving dish. "Pumpkin Pies" are appreciated in Burrillville. Hasty Pudding, the Muscovado, New Cheese and Apple Sauce, Pumpkin Pies and Sweetbread, these with the swine's flesh aforesaid, and a mug of cider or a glass of coffee, and our agriculturalist manages to make out a dinner.

In summer time we have a good many berries. These make a fine dish in a bowl of fresh milk. We have good wholesome milk, not the chalk and water beverage that dilutes the coffee of the metropolitan resident. Strawberries are found upon some of our hillsides, whortleberries are plenty. Let our city brethren smile if they will as they ride by our bushy pastures,—it is there we find the berries.

Our people are well but coarsely clad. The workmen around the village are mostly arrayed in the flimsy product of the slop-shop. We have several good tailors who will use good stock and have it well put together for their patrons who can afford it. The farmers wear coarse shirts, many of them are indifferent about the collar, whether it is Byronic or a la Greely; their strait vests have plain buttons and big pockets; their pants and overalls are made for service; cowhide boots defy mud, water and snakes, and with a heavy frock, Kossuth hat and buckskin mittens, their toilet is complete, and they sally forth to the field or the forest.

In a congregation here upon a Sunday, one may see coats of all patterns, from the style of a quarter of a century ago to the latest fashion. Our factory girls are fond of finery. Many of them give all their earnings for dress. It is true they look very pretty with ribbons and jewels and feathers, but the countenances of the young men fall when they compute the expense of such an establishment for a series of years. Our Burrillville girls are pretty amid all the mutations of fashion, but will not modest worth in a plain garb secure the best hearts the matrimonial market affords?

Our farmers wives and daughters have warm plaids in winter, pretty calicoes in summer, and sometimes silks and satin. What we shall eat and wherewithal we shall be clothed takes a good deal of our time, but we have long evenings and rainy days that we might devote to books and social improvement if the means were near to us.

We have but few books. As we have looked over the scanty

Burrillville: As It Was and As It Is by Horace A. Keach 1856

pile at the homes of many of our farmers, we have thought that a vast change would come over the spirit of their life when the school district and village libraries cultured among them a taste for good reading. The reforms that have been begun here will only be perfected by an education, that shall substitute the elevating pleasures of the intellect for the present craving for artificial stimulus to gratify unnatural appetites.

Some of our people ride in first class carriages. These are all single, there is only an occasional double family carriage in the town. Those who come out of the woods to meeting or to mill, often have rude, straight bodied unpainted vehicles that remind one of the car of Juggernaut.

Within a few years, chaise have revived, and those who patronize our liveries go bumping over our rough roads fully satisfied that a chaise is best because they have heard there grandmothers say that a "shay" was such "a nice thing to ride in." Well, a chaise has its advantages. Young men with patent leathers and fierce mustaches can fling back the top and travel from Brandy Hill to Round Top and from Round Top to Chepachet, and no one would imagine they were ever sober. They can be seen as well as though they had an open carriage, and then, if it rains and they are not too drunk, they can put up the top.

We have not much time for amusements, but we do have some recreation now and then. During the long evenings of winter, the young people make parties where the lads and lasses of the neighborhood are agreed in making the time fly merrily. They like to go to an old fashioned farmhouse where they can go "round the chimney." "Ring plays" are popular. These are known to everybody. They were common before the division of Glocester and will last a good while yet. Dancing is often introduced at these parties, and now and then a quiet game of whist. "Scorn," the "twenty questions," and the "stage coach" fill up the hours until the old folks want to go to bed and then the good humored company pack themselves in their sleighs, and a galloping drive by moonlight brings them to their homes.

Sometimes a sleigh ride is contrived by daylight and a great many people go to the city or Mendon or Douglas. The "old married folks" have "quilting parties" occasionally. They meet to sew together little bits of calico, and at the same time take the characters of their neighbors to pieces. They usually stay to tea, and the gossips grow garrulous as they scatter scandal they have kept for a whole week for want of so good an opportunity as they knew the "quilting bee" would afford, to retell it.

It was once the custom for the farmers to combine labor and amusement in the same way by meeting to husk each others corn. But these husking frolics are rare of late years, and all the romance of the "king ear" belongs to the poetry of labor of bygone time. Each man garners his own harvest, and "the rich plum pudding" and "sweet mince pie" are eaten in moody solitude. Sometimes our men go to Buck Hill to hunt rabbits. There are times when the woods swarm with them, and the skillful hunter usually carries a good stock home for his table. The route is long and hard, the cold sometimes becomes intense, and the tired company can scarcely drag one foot after the other when they come home; but the excitement of the chase is such that the next good day at early dawn, they are seen plodding past "Eagle Peak" to greet the rising sun on the summit of the bosky hill.

We have sometimes gone abroad to seek amusements that we might have found at home. We have always "lotted" on going to the "shore" each season after haying, but this summer a company went to the beach at Wallum Lake. Here they had a "Clam Bake." They found it far less wearisome and less expensive, too, than going to the shore below Providence.

When our labors and our amusements are over, they lay us to sleep in the family burial place. It is a custom here to have a little spot on each farm set apart as a place for graves. No sooner do we cross the line into the town of Douglas or Uxbridge than we find large churchyards. But the relatives of our families are often brought hundreds of miles that they may be laid with their fathers upon the old homestead. These little tithes of "God's acre" are not often visited. Friends go there to consign their dear ones to the dust or to place beside their grave the flowers they loved. In some of the older yards we find slate headstones, often broken, and the record entrusted to their keeping perchance illegible.

There are melancholy moods in all our lives when we prefer the willow shade of these silent retreats to the glare and bustle of this fitful life. It will be well, if, when our pulseless forms repose beneath the tree affection planted, a friend, whose sorrow has no tears, bends over us to read our name and turning away mournfully whispers, "We will love him again in Heaven."

Burrillville: As It Was and As It Is by Horace A. Keach 1856

SUPPLEMENT

At the monthly meeting of the Standing Committee of the Rhode Island Society for the Encouragement of Domestic Industry, Oct. 15 1856. Upon the petition of Horace A. Keach, Esq., setting forth that he is preparing a History of the town of Burrillville, and that he is desirous of annexing thereto the present statistics of that town as embodied in a report of said statics taken by him during the last summer under the direction and at the expense of General Dyer,

It was voted that the Secretary furnish Mr. Keach with a copy of his said report for the purposes aforesaid. A true copy, Attest, Wm. R. Staples, Sec'y.

To Gen. Elisha Dyer.
Dear Sir:
I have completed the task assigned me and upon the following pages may be found the results of my labors, the statistics of the town of Burrillville. They were procured by personal application to the inhabitants. Every farmer has given me the particulars of the farm occupied by him, so have the manufacturers, and mechanics generally the particulars of their business.

The aggregate of these makes the report here presented. So far as relates to agricultural crops and supplies, product of mills, and other similar points, the report, unless otherwise noted, refers to the year 1855.

The Educational statistics were obtained from the report of the school committee for the same year and various other sources. For the valuation of the town, reference was had to the town clerk's office and the records of the assessors of taxes. Other important facts herein stated have also been derived from the same source. It may be proper to state that neither officers nor individuals have shown any reluctance in affording the information required; it being however expressly understood that only the aggregates should be made public. I ought perhaps also to add that I found no disposition to overrate or underrate, but on the contrary, a desire that Burrillville should appear as it is.

Such has been my wish in executing the task assigned me, and having consulted on every point the most correct and reliable means of ascertaining the truth within my reach, and being conscious of no motive to misrepresent in any particular, I hand you the following report of my labors as containing a true statement of the statistics of Burrillville.

Hoping that the results may be acceptable to you and trusting that when published they may incite the inhabitants of Burrillville to still greater exertions for further progress in intelligence, in business, and in morals, I remain, Very Respectfully, Your Obedient Servant, Horace A. Keach.

STATISTICS OF BURRILLVILLE

Agricultural Statistics
Land - 1855
Acres

Woodland	16,262
Underwater	1,500
Waste land	300
In roads	421 3/4
Occupied by Buildings	30
Occupied by stone wall	94 1/4
In Gardens	200
Under the plough	2,039
Pasture Land	7,467
Meadowland	5,754
Total	34,068 Acres
Value of Land	$535,081

Fences
Rods

Wood Fence	105,530
Stone Wall	86,480
Total	192,010

Drains and Ditches
Rods

Covered Drains	3,640
Open Ditches	5,347
Total	8,987

Produce of Land - Natural Fruits

We have a good many berries: whortleberries, billberries, blackberries, and thimbleberries are plenty. A few strawberries grow in our pastures and old fields. In the woods on Buck Hill, a man may pick two quarts of whortleberries in an hour. We are so far from Providence that few are sent to the city. Scattered over the town are a few nut trees. There are about half a dozen Old English walnut and a score or two of butternuts; chestnuts are plenty. The ordinary pig walnut is common in our open pastures. We cultivate but few grapes. Now and then a small vine is seen in the yard of a farmhouse. There are some wild grapes in our woods. Around Wallum Lake they are found in considerable quantities and of the sweetest quality. Like the ivy that creeps over the crumbling columns of some old ruin, they cluster around the mossy material of our granite ledges and envelope the decaying lines of the old stone wall on many a neglected farm. They weave their emerald festoons around the delicate limbs of the trim larch, and drop their purple clusters into the crystal waters of our "sedgy brooks."

Wood Land

Cords of Wood sold	8,500
Tons Ship Timber	7
Cords Tan-bark	73
Thousands Hoop-poles	27
Thousands Feet Lumber	408
Thousands Shingles	1,582
Bushels Charcoal	68,100
Number Saw-mills	10
Number Shingle-mills	3

We have several old saw-mills and shingle-mills not in operation. As the timber is cleared away near them, those farther in the woods do the work. The name of our largest forest is Buck Hill Woods, estimated to contain 6000 acres.

Gardens

We are so far from the metropolis that we have no market gardens. A few of our farmers sell a little produce at the villages. Most of the families at the factories have gardens of their own. Among the esculent roots, beets, carrots, parsnips and onions are raised only in the garden. We do not cultivate these as a field crop nor have we any broomcorn or hops in our fields. A few currant and raspberry bushes circle around our garden borders, yet we make but few gills of currant wine. Raspberry jam is an occasional treat at the table of our farmers. A few feet are sometimes devoted to a strawberry bed, but this luscious luxury is enjoyed only by a few of the most refined. In our back woods in former times, the leisure that might be devoted to the culture of this best of fruits was given to that nauseous weed *tobacco*. It was planted on old coalpit beds, and in little patches where a fire had run over newly cleared land. But our chewers and smokers at the present time depend upon the southern article for their supply.

Tillage Land

	Acres	Bushels	Tons Fodder
Maize	586	12,782	511
Oats	600	12,000	200
Wheat	8	72	2
Barley	13	138	7
Rye	297	2,384	100
Millet	15	30	38
Buckwheat	92	649	26
Sowed Corn	4	--	15
Potatoes	602	46,800	
Turnips	10	1,600	
Beans	7	108	

Number of Grist Mills - five.

Pasture Land

The experiment of soiling cattle has scarcely been made in this town. Our stock roams over large pastures, often far into the woods. Many farmers let their cattle into their meadow lands in the fall to gnaw down the grass closely and materially injure the crop of the next year.

Meadow Land

	Acres	Tons
English Hay	5,120	2,403
" " & Timothy, Redtop, Etc.	4,670	1,953
" " & Clover	450	450
Natural Meadow	634	584
		Bushels
Redtop and Bent Seed	--	106
Cranberries	70	1,166

Fruit Cultivated

	Acres	Trees	Bushels	Bbls. Cider
Apples	364	15,490	15,350	795
Pears		107		
Peaches		628		
Plums		30		
Quinces		582		
Cherries		424		

The apple crop of last season was very small. We have no other fruit trees by the acre. A few years since we had two or three poor apologies for nurseries, but they are going to decay.

Fertilizers

Cords Barnyard Manure	1772
Cords " " made under cover	303
Cords Compost	135
Tons Plaster	41
Barrels Poudrette	83
Tons Guano	3 1/2
Tons Super-phosphate	- 3/4

Our farmers use a good many bushels of leached ashes. We have not been able to get any satisfactory returns of the amount. We have one soap factory and some are brought from the neighboring towns.

Stock - Horses

Stallions over 3 years	2
Mares over 3 years	99
Geldings over 3 years	237
Stallions under 3 years	7
Mares under 3 years	2
Geldings under 3 years	2
Total	349

Most of the horses used to transport freight to and from the city are kept out of town halfway to the city of Providence.

Horned Cattle

Cows over 3 years	652
Oxen over 3 years	354
Beeves	103
Bulls from 3 mos. to 3 years	27
Cows from 3 mos. to 3 years	65
Oxen from 3 mos. to 3 years	59
Calves killed	526
Devon Oxen	4
Durham Cows	3

Sheep

Over 1 year	186
Lambs	146
Pounds Wool (middle quality)	463
Fine wool Sheep	7

Swine

Over 1 year	464

Burrillville: As It Was and As It Is by Horace A. Keach 1856

Pounds Pork	135,315
Pigs raised	217

Poultry

Gallinaceous Fowls	3527
Turkeys	576
Geese	55
Ducks	27
Guinea Fowls	42
Produce of Poultry Yard	$1,973

Bees

Pounds Honey	799
Pounds Beeswax	40

Dairy

Pounds Butter	52,860
Gallons Milk	456,400

Our farmers make little cheese except for family consumption. They keep no account of that and it is impossible to estimate the amount.

Agricultural Implements

Horse Powers	6
Hay Cutting Machines	194
Fanning Mills	18
Corn Shellers	13
Value of Implements	$18,945

By the implements valued above, we intend such as are employed for agricultural purposes.

Laborers Employed in Agriculture

Men by the Year	40
Wages by the year	$7805
Women by the Year	16
Wages by the Year	$1664
Men by the Month	90
Average Wages per Month	$15

Our farmers do much of their work themselves. In the summer season the boys who are large enough to labor are kept from school to aid in the labors of the farm. We almost daily hear some farmer complain of being obliged to labor so hard, and they sigh for easier terms of western life. Our farmer's wives love to work, and their daughters are trained to domestic employments.

Burrillville: As It Was and As It Is by Horace A. Keach 1856

Buildings

Number of Houses	451
Number of Barns	287
Other Buildings	330
Value Houses	$225,500
Value Barns	11,480
Value Other Buildings	6,600
Total Value of Buildings	$243,580
Houses of Wood	447
Houses of Stone	4
Houses out of Highway	34
Houses with Basement Story	30
Houses Unpainted	116
Houses Unoccupied	26
Buildings with Slate Roof	1
Buildings with Gravel Roof	7

In the valuation of buildings above, factory buildings and machine shops are not included.

Manufacturing - Cotton

No. Cotton Mills -(1 wood & 1 stone)	2
No. Spindles	4200
Lbs. Cotton used in 1855	300,000
Cords Wood	340
Gallons Oil	546
Value other Supplies	$2100
Yds. Printing Cloths Mfgd.	275,000
Lbs. Yarn Warps, etc.	215,000
Males Employed	34
Females Employed	30
Average Persons per Family	6
No. Tenements of Wood	25
No. Persons per Tenement	6
Tons Freight Annually	400

Manufacturing - Woolen

No. of Woolen Mills of Stone	7
No. of Woolen Mills of Wood	15
Lbs of Wool Consumed Annually	2,400,000
No. sets of Machinery	47
No. Looms	322
No. Yds. Fancy Cassimere	731,295
No. Yds. Satinetts	1,600,000

No. Tons Coal	800
No. Cords Wood	4500
Value of Dye Stuffs	$24,336
Value Other Supplies	$20,341
No. Gallons Oil	40,700
No. Males Employed	577
No. Females Employed	181
Average Wages Males per Month	$24.00
Average Wages Females per Month	$24.00
No. families in Villages employed	260
Average persons in Family	5 1/2
Amount Freight per Annum, Tons	4000
Value Goods Mfgd. Annually	$1,372,991

Protection Against Fire - Five of our mills are provided with force pumps and beside we have two small fire engines. We have one steam engine of 60 horsepower. It is connected with one of our woolen mills to supplement the water power.

Mechanic Arts

Axe Shop	1
Blacksmiths	11
Butchers	3
Box Makers	6
Boat Makers	1
Carpenters	17
Dentist	1
Engineer	1
Gunsmith	1
Hoe Factory	1
Harness Maker	1
Masons	7
Machinists	50
Millwrights	2
Milliners	2
Painters	5
Shoe Makers	18
Tailors	3
Wheelwrights	6

Scythe and Drawing Knife Factory

No. Scythes made Annually	3000 Dozen
No. Drawing Knives " "	500 Dozen
Tons Hard Coal used	200
Bushels Charcoal	2000

Burrillville: As It Was and As It Is by Horace A. Keach 1856

Tons Iron used	65
Pounds of Steel	14,000
Hands Employed	22

There are about forty coal baskets made annually, value $140.

Machine Shops

No. of Machine Shops	2
Capital	$20,000
Kind of Machinery Made	Spindles & Flyers
Lbs. of Steel used	93,000
Value of Materials used	$15,000
Bushels Charcoal	3,100
No. of Hands Employed	50
Value of Annual Product	$40,000

Traders - 1856

Name	Location	Kind
John S. Colwell	Oakland	Variety Store
Daniel S. Mowry	Harrisville	Variety Store
Jacob Lewis	Buck Hill Woods	Variety Store
John A. Brown	Graniteville	Variety Store
Oliver A. Inman	Mohegan	Variety Store
A. L. Foskett	Mapleville	Variety Store
Daniel S. Shumway	Laurel Hill	Variety Store
Sayles & Wood	Pascoag	Variety Store
George Esten	Pascoag	Variety Store
D. Andrews & Co.	Pascoag	Variety Store
L. D. Millard	Pascoag	Variety Store
W. Armitage	Pascoag	Grocery Store
J. Paine	Pascoag	Grocery Store
James Wade	Pascoag	Stove Depot
Haynes & Smith	Glendale	Variety Store
Wm. R. Waterman	Pascoag	Furniture Room

Livery Stables

Name	Location	No. of Horses
Jesse M. Smith	Oakland	5
Willard Darling	Glendale	3
Mason Darling	Harrisville	5
Warren Potter	Pascoag	12
——Kimball	Laurel Hill	4

Financial

No. Banks	1

Burrillville: As It Was and As It Is by Horace A. Keach 1856

Granite, Inc. June 1833
Amount Capital	$100,000.00
No. Acres in Poor Farm	125
Original Cost	$2,400.00
Estimated Value - 1856	$3,000.00
Value of Personal Property at Poor House by order of Council, 30th March, 1855	$646.67
No. Indigents in 1856, Sept. 1	9

A donation was made to the town in 1844 by will of Doct. Levi Eddy of Burrillville. The amount was $1000 interest only to be applied to the support of the poor. Our paupers were sold at auction in 1807 for $200.

Estimated value by Assessors	
of Real Estate in 1885	$1,028,661
of Personal Property in 1855	439,540
Total	$1,468,201

Amount Tax per centage	24 1/2 cents
Money Tax in 1855	$3,600
Highway Tax in 1855	1,500
First Highway Tax, 1807	500
First Poll Tax in 1807	33 cents
Money Tax in 1856	3,600
Total Value of Property in 1856	$1,472,255

Internal Improvements

No. Miles Road	103
No. Miles Stage	14
No. Miles Railroad	
Partially Completed	9
Proposed	10
No. Bridges 20 feet span	21
No. Hotels	2

Condition of Bridges - Good. Guide Posts - Bad. Town House - Medium.

We lack accommodations for the preservation of our public records. They have usually been kept at the dwelling house of the town clerk. We have no *safe*, and the calamity of fire might unsettle half the titles in town.

Education

No. School Districts	16

Burrillville: As It Was and As It Is by Horace A. Keach 1856

No. School Houses	16
Condition of Houses	Good
No. Male Instructors	8
No. Female Instructors	21
Average Attendance	
1854-1855	459
1855-1856	502
Amt. Money received from State	$1,495.70
Amt. Money Raised by Town	$600.00
No. Public Libraries	1
No. Volumes	850
No. School District Libraries	--
No. Reading Rooms	--
No. Literary Societies	3

Mapleville Lyceum at Mapleville for public discussions and lectures.
Harrisville Lyceum at Harrisville for debates and mental improvement.
Union Club at Laurel Hill for debates and mutual improvement.

No. of Lawyers	1
No. of Physicians	3
No. of Post Offices in 1856	4
Newspapers Taken -	
Dailies	19
Semi-weeklies	39
Weeklies	443
Semi-monthlies	18
Monthlies	76
Quarterlies	2

Religious Statistics

No. Freewill Baptist Congregations	4
No. Methodist Congregations	3
No. Friends Congregations	1
No. Episcopalian Congregations	1
No. Roman Catholic Congregations	1
No. Clergymen	6
No. Meeting Houses	6
Value Church Property	$8,450
Church Accommodation	1,500
Congregations meeting in Schoolhouses	4

The Roman Catholics have lately laid the foundation of a church at the village of Harrisville in the center of town. It is to be 40 feet by 65 and it is designed to complete it this autumn.

APPENDIX

To the courtesy of D. M. Salisbury, Esq., are we indebted for the following article, originally prepared for the "Providence Journal."

Census of Burrillville

Whole Population	3,538
Number of Males	1,851
Number of Females	1,687
Persons over 90 years of age	7
Persons between 80 and 90	21
Persons between 70 and 80	71

Eldest couple now living are John Williams and wife—he 91, and she 90,—have been married 73 years.

The family most distinguished for longevity is the Esten family, children of John and Lydia Colwell Esten. Their names and ages are as follows:

Joseph Esten - in his 99th year.
Joanna Inman - in her 97th year.
John Esten - in his 89th year.
Marcy Brown - in her 80th year.
Salome Buxton - in her 77th year.
Amey Inman - in her 74th year.

The three following children have died since 1848:
Jemima Buxton - in her 95th year.
Martha Inman - in her 93d year.
Henry Esten - in his 85th year.
Their father died aged 78 years.
Their mother died aged 86 years.
Their father's mother died aged 97 years.
Their mother's father died aged 97 years.

The Hon. John Esten is still a resident of this town. Has been justice of the peace 26 years; Member of the Court of Probate for 34 years. Has represented the town in General Assembly 6 years. Judge of the Court of Common Pleas 4 years. Has joined in marriage 137 couples. Has been a member of the Freewill Baptist Church of

Burrillville: As It Was and As It Is by Horace A. Keach 1856

this town between 30 and 40 years.

    Number of dwelling houses in this town 633
    Number of families in this town   657
    Population of Pascoag Village   1082
    Population of Mapleville   305
    Population of Harrisville   202
    The population in 1840 was between 1900 and 2000;
        Increase between 1500 and 1600.

Burrillville: As It Was and As It Is by Horace A. Keach 1856

A
Absalone Hill 39
Acote's Fort 31
Adams, John 35
Air Line 38, 39, 40, 72
Aldrich, Abel 57
Aldrich, Adin 57
Aldrich, Russel 33
Allen, Rev. Reuben 56, 57, 58
Alum Pond 63
Andrews, D. & Co. 89
Apollo Belvidere 62
Armitage, W. 89
Armstrong, Col. Elijah 30, 31
Armstrong, Nelson, Esq. 11
Arnold, Esquire 55
Arnold, Noah 36
Artwright, Richard 67

B
Baiting Pond 9
Ballou's (Old Paul Place) 25
Ballou, Jirah 34
Ballou, Joshua W. 42
Ballou, Rev. Adin 60
Baptist Church 16, 57
Barnard, Hon. Henry 42
Barnes, Mr. 55
Battey, Smith 24, 60
Bee Hive 46
Belgium 72
Bellows, Dr. 36
Bicknell, Joshua 30, 31
Black Hut 10
Blackstone River 64
Blackstone Canal Co. 63
Boston 39
Bowen, Elder 58
Bowles, Elder Charles 56
Branch Bridge 15
Branch River 63, 64
Branch, Elder 57
Brandy Hill 14, 22, 64, 79
Bristol, RI 24
Britt, Elder 58
Brown, George 55
Brown, Harvey P. 47
Brown, John 37, 80
Brown, Marcy 92
Brown, Mr. 53
Brown, Nicholas, Esq. 57
Brown University 32
Buck Hill 14, 34, 36, 37, 72, 80, 82
Buck Hill Woods 22, 26, 83, 89
Bullard, Andrew 55
Bullock, Elder 56
Burleigh, Charles 49
Burleigh, Geo. S., Esq. 49, 59
Burlingame, Asa 34, 55
Burnham, Rev. Geo. 59
Burrell, Elder John 56
Burrill, Hon. James 32
Burrillville 9, 14, 15, 17, 19, 20, 21, 22, 23, 24, 29, 30, 32, 33, 35, 38, 39, 42, 43, 45, 46, 47, 48, 49, 52, 53, 55, 60, 62, 64, 67, 70, 72, 73, 75, 77, 78, 81, 90, 92
Burrillville Meeting House 21, 56, 59, 60
Buxton, Jemima 92
Buxton, Salome 92
Byronic 78

C
California 39, 75
Canada 49
Catholicism 49
Chandler, Dr. 24
Charleston, SC 56
Chase, Captain 75
Cheney, Elder 57
Chepa's Sack? River 11
Chepachet River 9, 63
Chepachet, RI 17, 18, 22, 29, 38, 64, 67, 79
Chickaseen River 12
Clarke, Joseph O. 44
Clear River 10, 11, 63
Colby, Elder John 55, 56
Colwell 36

Colwell, John S. 89
Connecticut 29, 64
Cook, Esquire 55
Cooper's Den 23
Cooper, Eddy 68
Cooper, Moses 11, 53
Cooper, Stephen 23
Copeland, Lyman 42
Cowen, Rev. 59
Crossman, Elder 56
Curtis, Justice 48

D
Danforth, Clarisa 56
Darling, Elder Jacob 56
Darling, Mason 89
Darling, Willard 89
Darned Man 37
Davidson, M. H. 57
Deep Cove 63
Den Hill 13
DeTocqueville, M. 5
Dorr 17
Douglas Meeting House 58
Douglas Turnpike 34, 38
Douglas Woods 38, 72
Douglas, MA 9, 14, 18, 34, 58, 79, 80
Dudley, Paul 19
Durfee, Elder Augustus 57
Dyer, Gen. Elisha 81

E
Eagle Peak 14, 46, 80
Eames, Rev. J. H. 59
East Greenwich 73
Eastern Indies 40
Eddy, Dr. Levi 11, 34, 90
Episcopalian 91
Esten Neighborhood 57
Esten, George 89
Esten, Henry 92
Esten, John 20, 21, 32, 92
Esten, Joseph 92
Esten, Lydia Colwell 92

F
Fairfield, Elder Smith 56
Fauquier, Wm. M. 56
Fenner, Governor 17
First Baptist Church 55
First Freewill Baptist Church 56
Fish, Rev. Mr. 60
Florida 70, 71
Forey, Samuel, MD 71
Forger's Cave 23
Fort Stanwix 15
Foskett, A. L. 89
Foss, Col. S. S. 43
Fox and Penn 69
Fox, Rev. Samuel 59
Freewill Baptists 91, 92
French War 10, 15
Friends 69, 91
Fugitive Slave Law 52
Fuller, Elder Willard 57

G
Gano, Dr. 55
Gleason, Mr. 55
Glendale 23, 89
Glocester/Gloucester, RI 9, 28, 29, 30, 32, 34, 52, 79
Granite Bank, Inc. 90
Graniteville 63, 89
Grassy Cove 63
Greely 78
Green Mountains 62

H
Halifax 39
Hammond, Rev. Chas. 59
Hampton Beach 62
Harriman, David P. 42, 57
Harrington, Dr. Christopher C. 36, 46
Harris, A. F. 48
Harris, Amaziah 32
Harris, Miss Catharine 75
Harrisville 18, 36, 37, 42, 46, 48, 59, 63, 89, 92

Burrillville: As It Was and As It Is by Horace A. Keach 1856

Harrisville Lyceum 91
Hartford Turnpike 39
Haynes & Smith 89
Herring Pond 10, 14, 53
Herring Woods 15, 36
Hopedale Comm. of
   Restorationists 60
Hopkins, Zebedee 20, 29
Horace 38, 69
Horse Head Woods 13
Hunt's Mill 15
Hunt, Seth 29
Huntsville Emporium 58
Hurl Gate 40

I
Inman, Amey 92
Inman, David 10
Inman, Francis H. 42
Inman, Joanna 92
Inman, John 9
Inman, John the first 18, 53
Inman, Martha 92
Inman, Oliver A. 80
Iron Mine Brook 10, 64

J
Jack the slave 53
Jack's Grave 53
Jefferson, Thomas 35
Jordan, Elder Zacharia 56

K
Keach, Eddy, Esq. 34
Keach, Horace A. 1, 81, 82
Keep, Calvin S. 23
Key West 71
Killingly, CT 56
Kimball, ——— 89
King George 2nd 14, 52
King Philip 9
King, Mr. 55
Knowles, John P., Esq. 47

L
Lake Erie 15

Lamb, Elder George 56
Lapham, Levi 32
Laurel Hill 59, 63, 89
Lee, Elder Richard 56
Lewis, Jacob 89
Long Cove 63
Lord, D. H. 57
Lyon, Rev. E. A. 59

M
Macready, Rev. Charles 59
Maine Law 33, 34, 48
Mann, Thomas 30, 31
Manton Library 42, 43
Maple Sap Swamp 9
Mapleville 36, 41, 46, 50, 53,
   59, 60, 63, 67, 68, 70, 89
Mapleville Lyceum 91
Marks, Elder David 56
Marsh, George W., Esq. 59
Massachusetts 18, 30, 34, 48,
   62
McKenzie's Stage 39
Mehunganug Swamp 11
Mendon 79
Metaka Woods 12
Methodism 58
Methodist 91
Methodist Episcopal Church 59
Millard, L. D. 89
Millerism 57
Miskianza River 11
Mississippi River 63
Missouri River 63
Mohawk Indians 10
Mohegan 10, 89
Mount Hope 9
Mount Pleasant 14
Mowry's Hall 47
Mowry, Benjamin, Jr. 47
Mowry, Daniel S. 89
Mowry, Jeremiah 55
Muddy Brook 24, 60

N
Narragansetts 9, 11

New England 40, 49, 60, 62, 71, 78
New Hampshire 55, 56, 57
New Hampton Biblical Inst. 57
New York 15, 39, 49, 57
Newport 22, 39, 60, 62
Nichols, Joseph 67
Nipmuc Indians 9, 13, 14, 24
Nipmuc River 90
Norfolk, VA 56
North Hill 63
North Scituate, RI 56
Northbridge 60

O
Oak Hill 53
Oakland 63, 89
Oatley, Elder 57
Olney, James 32
Olney, Jason, Esq. 53
Olneyville 18
Oregon 40
Owen, Brown 75
Owen, Thomas, Esq. 30

P
Pacific Road 40
Paine, Asa 42
Paine, Bazaleal 29
Paine, J. 89
Paine, John 23
Paine, Moab 32, 58
Parsonsfield, ME 56
Pas-co-ag Indians 10
Pascoag 9, 16, 17, 21, 25, 38, 39, 46, 50, 53, 57, 63, 64, 73, 75, 89
Pascoag Baptist Society 57
Pascoag River 14
Paulson's shingle mill 15
Pawtucket 24
Pequod 10
Phetteplace, Esek 19
Phillips place 17
Pilgrim Fathers 11

Pine Swamp 10
Pine Woods 18
Plymouth 11
Point Judith 40
Potter, Warren 89
Providence 10, 13, 15, 18, 24, 38, 39, 47, 53, 67, 70, 73, 80, 83
Putnam Pasture 36
Putnam, Joktan 29, 32, 36
Putnam, Joseph 37

Q
Quakers 60

R
Reed Swamp 64
Rhode Island 28, 32, 34, 60, 64, 70, 77
Rhodes, Capt. William 14, 37, 55
Rhodesville 14, 21, 36,
Rice, Joseph 30, 31
Robinson, Christopher, Esq. 47
Rocky Point 39
Roman Catholics 91, 92
Ross, William 32
Round Pond 22
Round Pond Brook 10
Round Top 15, 48, 79

S
Salisbury, Arnold & D. 10
Salisbury, Deacon Duty 11, 15, 16, 18, 20, 21, 53, 55, 92
Salsbury, Edward 15, 55
Sandwich Isles 40
Saxon Vale 63
Sayles & Wood 89
Scituate 28
Searles, Elder Ebenezer 56
Shay's Rebellion 17
Shays, Daniel 18
Shippee Bridge 10
Shockalog 9
Shumway, Daniel S. 89

Slater, John 67
Slatersville 67
Smith's Academy 43, 48, 57, 67, 68
Smith, Coomer, Esq. 43
Smith, Daniel 55
Smith, Daniel, Jr. 32
Smith, Jesse M. 89
Smith, John 13
Smith, Martin 36
Smith, Nelson 42
Smith, Paul 25
Smith, Pitts 32
Smith, Rufus 36, 43, 67
Smith, Samuel 32
Smith, Simeon 55
Smith, Solomon 36, 42, 55, 67
Smith, Urania 13
Smith, Zadoch 67
Smithfield, RI 15, 28, 60, 72
Smithville 9, 36, 43, 73
Snake Hill 11
Solitary Hill 28
South Carolina 37
South Kingston 11
Springfield, VT 56
Stanstead Plain 62
Staples, Wm. R. 81
Steere, Esq. 55
Steere, Isaac 42
Steere, Judge 17
Steere, Shadrach 24
Steere, Simeon, Esq. 30, 32
Stone, Lucy 53
Stout Raymond 19
Sucker Pond 14
Sutton, Vermont 37
Sweet, Elder David 56

T
Taber, Mr. 75
Taft, Charles 37
Tar Kiln River 67
Tar Kiln Saw Mill 13, 43
Temperance 47

Thayer, Dr. Enoch 34
Thayer, Mr. 55
Thompson, CT 9, 14, 26, 64
Thompson, Lewis 67
Thurber 67
Tourtelott, Daniel 29
Tourtelott, Jesse 30, 31
Town House 21, 55
Triptown 28

U
Unadilla, NY 37
Union Club at Laurel Hill 91
Universalists 60
Uxbridge, MA 9, 10, 34, 80

V
Vermont 69

W
Wade, James 89
Wakefield Saw Mill 64
Waldron, Edmund 29
Walling, Elder Joseph 57
Walling, George, Esq. 21
Wallum Lake 9, 14, 15, 38, 62, 63, 73, 80, 83
Wallum Pond 63
Warren 73
Washington 39, 46
Waterford 38
Waterman, Benjamin 30
Waterman, Wm. R. 89
Webster 64
Weeks, Rev. James 57, 59
Wesley, John 55, 58
West India Isles 37, 45
Westcott, Rev. Mr. 58
Wethersfield, VT 56
White School House 48, 57
White, Captain Samuel 11
White, Elder Joseph 56
White, John 34
White, Samuel, Esq. 11, 63
Whitfield 55
Wilkinson, David 63

Wood, Smith, Esq. 10, 37
Wooding, Rev. G. W. 59
Woodman, Elder Jonathan 56
Woodstock 64
Woonasquatucket 38, 39, 72
Woonsocket 39, 43, 47, 48, 67, 73
Woonsocket Falls 48
Woonsocket Union 38
Worcester, MA 19

X

Y
Young, Othniel 37
Young, Peleg 34

Z

www.ingramcontent.com/pod-product-compliance
Lightning Source LLC
Chambersburg PA
CBHW071737090426
42738CB00011B/2515